wine
wisdom

Susy Atkins

wine
wisdom

Special photography by **Tim Winter**

Quadrille

First published in 2004 by
Quadrille Publishing Limited
Alhambra House
27–31 Charing Cross Road
London WC2H 0LS

Editorial director Jane O'Shea
Creative director Helen Lewis
Project editor Lisa Pendreigh
Editor Jane Keskeys
Senior designer Jim Smith
Photographers Tim Winter, Charmaine Grieger
Food stylist Emma McIntosh
Props stylist Wei Tang
Production Rebecca Short

Cataloguing in Publication Data: a catalogue record for this book
is available from the British Library.

ISBN 1 84400 117 2

Printed in Singapore

Contents

Introduction

How the world of wine has changed! Imagine being a wine drinker in the 1960s or '70s (and if you were, cast your mind back), when almost all the wine in the shops came from the classic regions of France, Germany, Italy and Spain, and a lot of it was very poor quality indeed. The shelves groaned with oxidised, off-dry, insipid whites and rough, nasty, under-ripe reds. Sickly-sweet wines were commonplace, along with cherry liqueur and advocaat.

Of course, there were great clarets (red Bordeaux), burgundy and port from the top vintages, but hardly anyone could afford to splash out on such delights. Wine was the preserve of the upper-classes, and even there, only the men took a real interest. If your father had a cellar of fine wine then you might inherit his hobby, buying your bottles from a crusty, venerable London wine merchant, but if you were an 'ordinary' drinker, you probably stuck to beer, perhaps with the odd bottle of Rioja or sherry on very special occasions.

Fast forward to today, and a quick browse of the modern supermarket shelf reveals an extraordinary array of wines from right across the globe. Chile, South Africa, New Zealand, even Uruguay, Canada and Morocco, now provide us with vinous delights. Even better, those classic clarets, ports and so on are still turning up regular treats, and producers in Europe are under more pressure than ever to keep up with the competition. OK, not every bottle is utterly delicious, and standards of inexpensive wine could still be improved overall, but on the whole it is possible to buy enjoyable bottles of all styles and flavours on every high street without breaking the bank.

The vast majority of people are at it now – buying, drinking, enjoying and discussing wine. I'm not talking about the volume consumed, but the simple fact that a wide cross-section of the population enjoys a glass or two every now and again. Who hasn't been to a party recently where us 'ordinary' folk – men and women, young and old – were talking about the wine we were drinking? In my small rural village, there is even an informal wine club. It was set up by a group of enthusiasts, who meet up on a regular basis to crack open a few bottles and chat about them. They are certainly not elitists, and the wines they bring are not especially rare or expensive, but they are all developing a great love of the liquid.

It is this new enthusiasm for wine that got me thinking about a wine book that focuses on fun tastings. There are, of course, plenty of wine books on the shelves, from pocket books on fine vintages and annual lists of 'best buys' to tomes on food and wine matching and guides to wine regions. Most have their place. However, few books focus on the pleasures of tasting wine and the way this helps to build up knowledge, providing you with a sense of your own preferences. Too many wine books do the opposite, in fact. They tell you about soil, climate, grapes, and they sometimes tell you what you SHOULD be buying, but they don't help you to explore and develop your own individual taste.

This book does. Through a series of three 'stages' - from beginner, through intermediate, to advanced - it helps you discover the wine styles that suit you. A wide range of styles is suggested, to try and contrast, to pit one against the other. It's then up to you to decide which ones you continue to explore, on what occasions, and with what food. This is all done through a series of eighteen wine tastings, designed to be tried at home.

The tastings are fairly general. There is no point in recommending you buy one specific wine (Château l'Ardtofind 1998), as it won't be in all the shops. Instead, I might recommend you buy an oaked white Bordeaux of a certain age and within a certain price bracket. Everyone should be able to find one of those, unless they live in Outer Mongolia (although, the way wine is going, they can probably get it there too). That said, don't worry if you can't find an exact match for every single wine suggested. Don't see the book's progression as too rigid either - if you want to dip in and out of the tasting exercises, then that's fine.

Tasting is definitely the 'hero' of this book, but it is impossible to appreciate wine without having some knowledge of vines, wine regions and methods of production. So in each of the three stages there is information on all of these subjects, which is designed to expand your knowledge a bit further, before the next set of tastings. There are some useful sections on how to buy, serve and store wine, too, and how to match it with food.

You can use this book to learn about wine on your own (it will cost you a bit in terms of bottles, but at least you don't have to shell out for an evening course), but I recommend you get together with your mates and turn at least some of your tasting exercises into a fun, lively, interactive wine party. Each person can bring along a different bottle, which will help with the cost, and after you have finished tasting, you can compare notes. Don't expect everyone to rate the wines exactly the same - no one has identical tastes in wine. That's the whole point - get tasting and discover exactly what is out there, and what really suits you!

stage 1

Here's where the journey towards wine wisdom begins! Kicking off with the lowdown on the six most important grape varieties, this is where you learn how to taste wine like a pro, discovering exactly what to look out for in a glass of vino. There is some introductory information on vineyards, wineries and how to buy, serve and match wine with food, too. Let's get going!

The big six

The main reason why wine styles vary so widely is the use of different grapes, or grape blends, which create their own flavours, aromas, textures and ageing potential. So one way to learn about wine is to learn about the major grape varieties.

Some grapes are only found in one or two regions of the world, while others have spread their tendrils across the winemaking globe. The six varieties introduced here are arguably the most important. They are internationally grown and internationally famous. Why? In the case of several, it's because they make consistently good wine, so both producers and drinkers are keen to try them. Or it is because they travel well, making quality wine effortlessly in many climates.

Their fame is for cultural and historical reasons too. Perhaps immigrants brought native vines with them when they moved overseas, or perhaps these vines made such a splash in prestigious wine regions that more far-flung areas wanted 'in' on the act. For example, Cabernet Sauvignon is so highly rated in Bordeaux that it's hardly surprising newer wine-producing areas have sought to emulate this success.

For all of these reasons and more, here are the most popular grapes – the ones that have caught our imagination most often down the centuries and created more award-winning, commercially successful, reliably delicious wines than any others.

Each is capable of producing great wine – when they thrive in good conditions, with the right climate and soil, before being turned into wine by a talented producer. This is not always the case, as plenty of dull Riesling, over-blown Chardonnay and under-ripe Cabernet proves, but they do have the *potential* to be world-beaters.

And each makes a range of wines at different prices – easy-drinking, inexpensive plonk, medium-priced, more impressive bottles and top-notch, cult classics. Other varieties are discussed in later stages, but for now, get to know The Big Six.

Chardonnay

If you haven't encountered Chardonnay, you must have been living on Mars for the past twenty years. Actually, there is probably a Chardonnay vineyard on Mars these days. This is a vine that pops up everywhere, from the great vineyards of Burgundy in France (for many, its true home), to vast tracts of Australia and Chile, to smaller pockets in Canada, Austria, even China and England.

Almost all white burgundy, from basic Bourgogne Blanc to prized Chablis and Montrachet, is made from 100% Chardonnay, although it doesn't always say so on the label – the Burgundians tell you the place the wine comes from, not the grape variety. It's also one of the three Champagne grapes, used for premium sparkling wine all over the world. The Italians love it, the Spanish are encouraging it (occasionally even using it for their sparkling wine, Cava), and the Californians worship it.

Most grape producers enjoy growing Chardonnay. It is so easy to grow, making palatable wine almost all the time. It behaves well in the winery, and can be crafted into fresh, lemony, unoaked wine or aged in barrels for big, rich, toasty styles, according to the winemaker's whim. True, it sometimes makes rather mundane, one-dimensional 'quaffing' white, but it is rarely horrid. At its best, it is sublime, with many complex characteristics of tropical fruit, citrus, cream, butter, nuts and honey.

Still, for most of us, over-oaked, richly cloying Chardonnay, where the fruit is dominated by a sawdusty, vanilla-drenched wood flavour, is unappealing. The nuances that Chardonnay picks up after time in oak barrels should be just that – nuances. Subtle and well-balanced, oak should enhance the wine, not overpower it. Around a decade ago, winemakers went over-board with oak, perhaps confusing their customers with hungry termites. Thankfully they are now checking themselves, and most modern Chardonnays rely on naturally juicy fruit flavours, with just a restrained note of wood/spice.

Experience the many faces of Chardonnay by trying examples from Burgundy (trade up from cheap basic Bourgogne Blanc to Chablis, Meursault or Puligny-Montrachet if someone else is paying!), and from the south of France (choose Vin de Pays d'Oc Chardonnay for a ripe, rounded bargain). Taste Austrian Chardonnay if you can – it's rare, but deliciously complex – and modern Italian or Spanish examples, from Tuscany or Sicily, Somontano or Navarra respectively. From the New World, put Australian, Californian, Chilean, New Zealand and South African Chardonnays on your list and compare.

Don't forget, most sparkling wines and Champagnes contain Chardonnay, so open some of those too (hint: Champagne labelled *blanc de blancs* is entirely made of Chardonnay). If you claim you 'don't like Chardonnay', be aware you're dismissing a grape that comes in many guises!

Sauvignon Blanc

Sauvignon Blanc is arguably the second most-loved of all the white varieties, and its popularity seems to be growing. Most people adore its mouthwatering grassy aroma and crisp citrus and gooseberry flavours. It's seen by some as less complex than Chardonnay, and it's probably true that the greatest Loire Valley Sauvignons are one-dimensional compared with the finest white burgundies, with simple fresh fruit and grassiness at the fore. But that doesn't mean Sauvignon is any less wonderful to drink – in fact, devotees say its elegance and refreshing purity puts it far above the potentially overwhelming riches of Chardonnay.

Enjoy tasting Sauvignon Blanc like a pro, as this grape has such a distinctive character – one that leaps right out of the glass and declares itself loudly. It always stands out in blind tastings (where the labels are covered) and it is deeply satisfying to swirl an unknown white wine in your glass, then smell it and think immediately: 'oh yes, Sauvignon Blanc!' Look out for lemons, gooseberries, freshly mown grass, even a hint of tomato or herbs.

There are, roughly, two main types of Sauvignon Blanc – the cooler-climate style epitomised in France, particularly in Bordeaux, where it is often blended with Semillon to make great classic whites, and in the Loire Valley, where the wines of Sancerre and Pouilly-Fumé are made from 100% Sauvignon (no need to say 'blanc' every time).

Then there's the New World style, which reaches its zenith in New Zealand. The distinctive Sauvignon character is still there in each hemisphere, but whereas French Sauvignons are restrained, bone-dry and crisp, it's as though New Zealand wines have had the volume turned up. The vibrant gooseberry, cut-grass and tomato vine aromas jump out and grab you by the throat. These are white wines that could never be described as subtle!

Try Sauvignon, too, from South Africa (which seems to achieve a clever balance between French and New Zealand styles), Austria (particularly crisp and racy), and cooler spots in Australia and Chile.

Riesling

Riesling gets a bad press from time to time as it is still associated with Germany's poorest, blandest white wines. But to most serious wine lovers, it remains one of the world's greatest grapes. It is derided by some, yet utterly desired by others. So let's get things straight – Riesling is NOT responsible for the pale, monotonous ocean of mediocre Liebfraumilch, Hock and Piesporter. Although these wines occasionally have Riesling in the blend, they're made using cheap, inferior grape varieties.

Instead, Riesling creates the greatest whites of Germany; naturally light, almost ethereal, Spring-like, apple-scented. Wines which range from crisply acidic and dry through riper, medium-sweet, to luscious, honeyed sweeties. If you are spending time exploring the world of wine, then getting to know German Riesling is an absolute must. Try to spot regional differences – for example, Mosel Rieslings tend to be light, floral and appley, while the Rheingau makes a fuller-bodied style, and so on. And try German Riesling both young and mature – partly because of its high acidity, this variety mellows beautifully into richer, aromatic older age and is worth cellaring for many years.

Riesling doesn't only make fine wine in Germany. Alsace, just across the border in eastern France, is another destination for lovers of serious, long-lived Riesling. Alsatian Riesling has more alcohol and a richer texture than German Riesling, but, as in Germany, the top winemakers here believe it expresses the character of an individual vineyard site, its climate and soil, more sensitively than any other variety, and they often craft it with great care and expertise.

While in Europe, don't miss the steely, bracingly fresh quality of Austrian Riesling – rare, but worth the search. Don't miss out on the lime-drenched, pithy pleasures of Australian Riesling, a much fruitier and riper version than Europe makes. Try Aussie Riesling from the Clare or Eden Valleys or Coonawarra (all regions in South Australia) for an immediate conversion to this grape. After this, if you still think it tastes like Liebfraumilch, I'll eat my hat!

New Zealand and Canada also turn out some serious, long-lived Rieslings, and do try the sweet styles from either country if you get the chance. In fact, you don't really know this grape until you've sampled a delectable, tangy, lime-marmalade flavoured dessert Riesling, quivering with fresh acidity.

Cabernet Sauvignon

It used to be easy to put Cabernet Sauvignon forward as the world's most popular, fashionable and highly regarded red grape. Now fruity young Merlot seems determined to usurp its crown, and Syrah (see section 2) is lurking in the background too. Even so, Cabernet remains much loved and it is pretty hard to find a bad word to say about it.

Why? Like Chardonnay, this is a variety that seems to make more palatable wine than most – it's a hardy grape which travels well and pops up all over the place, from Bordeaux to South Africa, Spain to Australia, California to Bulgaria. The hallmarks of a top Cabernet are a deep colour, a blackcurrant flavour and full-bodied weight and structure. It ages well in oak barrels, producing more spicy, cedary notes. Look out for chocolate, mint, leather and even lead-pencil hints on the more complex wines.

It blends with ease – mainly with Merlot, as the classic duo from Bordeaux, but also with Shiraz in Australia, with Sangiovese in Italy and with Tempranillo in Spain. Each time it brings to the partnership its forceful structure, rich cassis fruit, and deep hue. Or that's the idea, anyway. Obviously there are poor Cabernets out there (under-ripe, stalky-green ones that taste of runner beans certainly don't get my vote), but in general this is a star performer, often used to make the top or 'flagship' red of a winery, either alone or with the backing of a blending partner.

Fans of Cabernet claim it is still the most important grape in Bordeaux, although Merlot is in fact grown more widely in the area. But it is true that the long-lived and majestic wines of the famous Châteaux in Bordeaux's Médoc and Graves regions are based mainly on Cabernet, and even some of the cheaper wines of the region show that refined and rich character of the grape (though watch it at the 'bargain basement' end of the shelf). If you're a Francophile, do check out the ripe, rounded Cabernets of the deep South for good value too.

Italy has some serious, oaky Cabernets and Cabernet blends, and California Cabernet is also a must for the serious fan. Expect a big, powerful, chunky, impressive style of red from America's West Coast. The Australians make loads of Cabernet, ranging in style from easy-drinking, sweetly ripe Cabernet-Shiraz blends to very serious, blockbuster, multi-dimensional reds. A taste of some South African, Chilean and Argentinian Cabernets should give a fair snapshot of the rest of the world – of these, Chile's well-priced wines, bursting with juicy, freshly picked blackcurrant, are the most immediately appealing.

Merlot

Merlot is madly fashionable, and has been for several years now, so it is hard to remember that this variety used to hover dimly in Cabernet's shadow. Its softer, more generous, plummy character was mainly used to flesh out the austere Cabernet in blends, and it was under-appreciated in its own right.

Now trends have swung the other way, and Merlot is the red wine to order if you are a style-conscious drinker. Its new popularity is partly because this grape is often soft and easy to drink when young – unlike Cabernet, which usually needs time to lose its tannic edges – and there has been a general trend for fruitier, juicier wines of late.

It's also well-liked in the modern age of winemaking because it ripens in cooler spots than Cabernet, so it has been made successfully in lots of areas where other reds turned out under-ripe and stalky. New Zealand is a case in point – this cooler-climate wine country has moved away from Cabernet a bit and now makes more successful Merlot or Merlot-based blends than it used to.

In Bordeaux, Merlot can sometimes take centre stage in 'claret' – it creates some truly great and surprisingly full-bodied, long-lived wines in the St-Emilion and Pomerol areas – especially since there's been a dramatic upturn in quality over the past 20 years. Merlot is by far the main component of the blend (with Cabernet Franc and Cabernet Sauvignon) in these two areas. It is also grown very widely in the wider environs of Bordeaux, both as a partner for Cabernet and as the main grape behind plenty of cheap red claret, both tasty and terrible!

Outside Bordeaux, the South of France turns out some very attractive, ripe Vin de Pays d'Oc made from Merlot. There are some good-value, tasty bargains from Eastern Europe too, especially Bulgaria, and impressive bottles from both Italy and Spain.

The Americans take Merlot very seriously these days, producing powerful, chunky, often overtly oaky examples in California, Washington State and Long Island. Do try these, and Merlots from South Africa, Chile and Argentina. A passing trend, or the perfect wine for our times? Despite some over-inflated prices and hype, I think I'll call it the latter, but taste away and decide for yourself.

Pinot Noir

Unlike Merlot, Pinot Noir never seems to be 'in' or 'out', but it's often the subject of serious debate. The problem is its patchy quality. One minute it can seem a lovable wine, silky-smooth, juicy and aromatic, seductive and easy to love. The next bottle – even one from the same region or producer – might be dreadful, tart, under-ripe or dilute. Even its most adoring fans will agree that Pinot Noir is as difficult and moody as a two-year-old child, inspiring great joy and deep irritation in equal measure.

If that's not enough to put you off, I'm afraid fine Pinot is usually very costly. The top wines from Burgundy will set you back a small fortune, as will the best examples from the New World. So why bother? Well, as I said, this grape can produce stunning reds, quite unlike any other, particularly in texture – soft and juicy, slipping down like liquid velvet. The fresh, aromatic, sweet-strawberry fruit of youth gives way with age to wonderfully rich hints of chocolate, coffee, even earthiness and game. It goes terrifically well with red meat, game, quality cheeses and tomato pasta dishes. When it is good, Pinot is very, very good indeed.

You won't get to know it unless you try bottles of red burgundy (as with Chardonnay, don't expect to see the words Pinot Noir on the label, but almost all red burgundy is Pinot). The cheapest Bourgogne Rouge can be poor, so move up to wines from specific parts of the region such as Gevrey-Chambertin, Nuits-St-Georges or Pommard, but be prepared to shell out a lot for the best. Perhaps a slightly cheaper bottle labelled Givry or Mercurey (from the Côte Chalonnaise area) provides a less painful introduction, but as detailed above, Pinot Noir is never a completely safe bet.

Still in France, the Pinot Noir made in Alsace can be delightful, in a simple, tangy way. Try it lightly chilled with fresh salmon – one of the few successful marriages of red wine and fish. And out in the wider world, do try abundantly fruity, sometimes chocolate-coated Pinot Noir from Chile (often more reasonably priced, thank goodness), California and Oregon (both of which can be remarkably sophisticated), and New Zealand examples, with lots of lively cherry-berry flavours.

Pinot Noir is, like Chardonnay, one of the three grape varieties used for Champagne, and is used for sparkling wine in other corners of the globe. So, if you decide its unpredictable nature is putting you off the still wines, enjoy it in the form of fizz!

The vineyard

Think all vineyards are the same? Just rows and rows of plants trained on wires, all pruned carefully and sitting in the sun, popping out uniform bunches of grapes? Think again. I've stood in many vineyards around the world and can honestly say that the differences between them are quite marked – even when the grape varieties grown are exactly the same. The climate, the soil, the training and pruning system, the slope, the rainfall or irrigation method – these are just some of the factors that vary quite dramatically from one spot to another. So a Chardonnay vineyard in Burgundy looks quite different from a Chardonnay vineyard in Australia. Then again, a Chardonnay vineyard in Margaret River, Western Australia, might also be quite different from a Chardonnay vineyard in Padthaway, South Australia.

So what? Wine buffs find this fascinating, not (usually) because they are sad souls obsessed with soil types or wire trellises, but because these contrasts in location really do dictate a wine's character. Put another way, the conditions under which grapes are grown decide the flavours in your glass. Taste a particularly fine wine from a single vineyard site, and you are sampling the very essence of a particular piece of land... It simply wouldn't taste the same from any other spot on earth. The French have a quasi-mystical term to describe this sense of place that is stamped on a wine – *terroir*.

Of course, some wines reflect the *terroir* of a whole region rather than a single vineyard because grapes are sourced from a larger area, and many more (especially cheaper ones) are made from grapes sourced from more than one region (cross-regional blends), and so the influence of *terroir* is far less evident here. A few great wines are made like this (the grapes for one of Australia's greatest reds, Penfold's Grange, come from several different regions) but generally speaking, these wines tend to be less interesting than ones which show regional – and especially single-vineyard – character.

Location, location, location
One of the most interesting tasting exercises is a comparison of wines made from grapes grown a short

distance from each other – same grape, same winemaker, same conditions in the winery, same oak barrels, but definitely different results! Subtle shades of fruit flavour, a more aromatic note, a mineral hint, a longer life ahead – all these might reflect the different location where the vines stood. One vineyard might be on a steeper slope than another, for example. This means the sun hits the vines at a different angle, the rain drains away more quickly or slowly – even the harvesting might be done in a particular way. It all affects the liquid in your glass, however subtly.

The surrounding land is important too. Is the vineyard close to the sea? That will affect the area's climate (see below), and the salty air might influence the vines. Are there mountains close by, which might protect the vineyards from rain? The altitude is also important – high altitude means cooler conditions.

It is often claimed that a vineyard surrounded by eucalyptus trees will produce wine with a characteristic 'eucalypt' flavour, or that any vines growing close to Southern France's wild *garrigue* scrub pick up a little wild herbaceousness, or those next to a field of garlic might

Far left: Ancient vines basking in the hot sunshine at the Vega Sicilia estate in Ribera del Duero, Spain.

Above: A young Viognier vineyard flourishing in the Robertson region of South Africa.

have a certain pong to them! There may or may not be some truth in these claims, but nearby crops will influence the vineyard in that natural predators may be encouraged or repelled, and water supplies might be affected.

Climate control

In the first tasting that follows, you try two wines made from the same grape, one from a cool climate area, another from a warmer place. You can't fail to notice a huge difference between the two, and this is true of all wines that are made in areas with contrasting climates. Cooler vineyards produce wines with higher acids (tasting fresher, crisper, more mouthwatering) and, often, lower alcohol levels, while grapes from warmer places get very ripe, and the wines tend to be richer, powerful, full-bodied and alcoholic.

Vines trained up high on pergola trellises, to raise them up above the damp ground.

Most winemakers champion vineyards in places that get lots of warm sun by day, but where the temperatures are much cooler at night. This produces grapes with good levels of ripeness, but the colder nights help them retain a fresh acidity. The Marlborough region, on New Zealand's South Island, is a good example of a place with this type of climate.

Low humidity is also important as too much damp can lead to rot and disease in the vines. A fresh breeze is good for keeping the vines healthy, but constant wind, or heavy storms, can damage the vines.

When connoisseurs talk about good versus poor vintages, they are referring to the weather in particular years. Most wine is made in areas that have some fine years and some not-so-fine - frost, hail, lack of warm sun, rain during the late summer and autumn, extreme heat - all can lead to poor wine, even in a region with the potential to make great wine. If you are splashing out on expensive wine, it pays to do a bit of research into the best vintages. See page 102 (Stage Three, In the vineyard) for a few tips here, or invest in a brand-new pocket guide devoted to worldwide vintage comparisons for a comprehensive scan.

Down to earth

It may be surprising to discover that a conscientious vinegrower supplying a winery is NOT looking for fertile, perfect soils. Not nearly as much as a grower supplying a green-grocer with table grapes. The aim for wine is not to harvest a plentiful crop of big, juicy grapes, but to produce fruit with lots of flavour and character, which tends to mean smaller, thicker-skinned grapes that contain less water. Lower yields mean the vines put more flavour into the grapes, so ironically, small crops are often exactly what's needed. The soil should make the vine struggle a bit to produce its crop, and many great vineyards are based in fairly poor soils. That's why many cheap and bland wines are made from high-cropping vineyards grown on fertile plains!

Vines need to be well-drained, as water-logged soils cause problems. Otherwise, soils vary enormously - they might have high limestone content, or lots of big rocks, or they might be flinty or based on glacial deposits. Certainly some of the character of a soil rubs off on the wine – limestone seems to produce particularly fine Chardonnay, for example, while the big stones sitting on the surface of certain vineyards absorb and reflect the sun's heat, producing richer, riper reds, as in Châteauneuf-du-Pape. More examples of soil type dictating wine style will crop up later on in this book.

Training course

It's not a subject to bang on about endlessly unless you need a cure for insomnia, but trellising (most vines are trained on wires) is important too. There are several different types of system. Some vines are untrained, and sit in bushes close to the ground. There are plenty of bush vines in warmer parts of Spain, and in South Africa, for example. There's a good reason for this, as it usually happens in hot climates where the bush canopy protects against moisture loss. It's cheaper than training the plants.

In particularly damp areas, such as Galicia in western Spain, the vines are trained up high, away from wet ground and potential rot. In other areas, for example, cooler parts of New Zealand, it's more important to separate the canopy of leaves using wires to let air and sun in and expose the grapes so they reach full ripeness.

Pruning

Again, the way a vineyard is pruned varies from place to place, and from grower to grower. The aim is to produce the healthiest, ripest grapes, and ones with the most flavour. To this end, the plant's shoots are trimmed back in the spring, to stop the vine growing wildly and producing too many leaves, but some of the developing bunches of grapes might be cut off later in the season, too, to reduce the harvest and make sure the quality of the remaining bunches is high. In some places, the canopy of leaves is cut back – exposing the grapes to more sun and air. This is called 'canopy management' and is adopted in regions with cooler climates where there is a danger the grapes won't get ripe enough.

Harvesting

Some vineyards are harvested by machines and some by hand. It is often a matter of convenience – steeply terraced vineyards, such as those in Portugal's Douro Valley (port country), are almost impossible to harvest by machine, so the vineyard workers are sent in with their secateurs. Machine harvesting is cheaper, but some argue that it produces a less perfect crop than hand selection.

A lot of thought goes into the perfect time to pick. Grape growers check out the ripeness levels of their fruit until they are satisfied the moment is right. The weather forecast might be taken into account too – no one wants to see their unpicked fruit left on the vine as a week of heavy rain and storms approaches. Sometimes the harvesting is done at night – I'll never forget the surreal experience of sitting on a huge harvesting machine in Australia, trailing up and down floodlit vineyards at 3am!

The reason for night harvesting is that the grapes are picked while the temperatures are cool (important in a hot climate) so they remain in better condition on the way to the winery. These days, the importance of keeping the grapes in prime condition is well understood. No one wants bruised and oxidised grapes arriving at the winery. Because of this, small containers are used to collect the fruit, and sometimes the crushing is actually done on site at the vineyard, so the juice is removed straight after picking. But usually the fruit is taken to the winery as quickly as possible. Which is where we are going next...

In the winery

Now the fruit has appeared at the winery, ready to be turned into wine. What makes the difference at this stage? Why do some winemakers win top awards time after time, while some become known for turning out lots of cheap palatable plonk, and others merely produce pig swill? In other words, how can humans dictate the style and quality of wine once the grapes are picked?

Put very simply, wine is just fermented grape juice, its sugar turned to alcohol. It's not tricky to get juice to do that – in fact, it does it more or less on its own if it has enough natural yeast and the temperature is right. But making it taste good is something else. Just as an apple or banana will turn brown when exposed to air, so wine will oxidise unless it is vinified carefully and protected from air.

Conditions in the winery should be hygienic – something modern winemakers understand much better than their ancestors. And keeping the juice cool is an important measure when making fresh, lively whites and rosés – think 'refrigeration'. Then there's the choice of container – stainless steel vats, cement tanks, or oak barrels? And choice of packaging – bottle or box, cork or screw-cap? These factors make more difference than you might expect.

So, there are many choices for winemakers and each one will affect the wine that results. Some words about all these basic decisions follow, but let's start with outlining the simple contrasts between making white, red and rosé wine.

Whites

White wine is generally made from the juice of white grapes, although very occasionally the clear juice of red grapes is run off and vinified to make white (try squeezing a red grape and you'll see the juice is transparent, not purple).

It's important to keep the juice fresh, with lively acidity, and fruity aromas and flavours, so modern winemakers are particularly keen to keep temperatures low during the process of winemaking (it's the same

The high-tech winery of Vergelegen, in South Africa, where new, temperature-controlled stainless steel tanks help to keep juice and wine fresh and cool.

principle as keeping salad crisp and fresh in the fridge). In an up-to-date winery, with modern equipment, white grapes tend to be crushed quickly after arriving in the winery, and the juice is run off and kept chilled in stainless steel containers.

Then it's fermented, usually with a yeast culture added, and during the fermenting process the low temperature is maintained. Some whites, however, are fermented in oak barrels to gain extra flavour from the wood – rich, toasty Chardonnays are sometimes made in this way.

When the yeast has done its work, turning sugar into alcohol, it dies and forms a sediment at the bottom of the fermenting container. This deposit is called the lees. Some whites, most famously the better quality Muscadets, are left on their lees – the words 'sur lie' on a bottle of French white indicate this has happened. Expect a more creamy, perhaps biscuity or bready character from contact with the sediment and occasionally a slight spritz in such wines. Some are even stirred so that the sediment adds extra flavour and aroma to the finished wine. Then the wine is filtered and either bottled, or put in oak barrels to mature (see below).

Reds

Reds are treated quite differently, because the colour, tannin and flavour from the skins are all needed. Tannins are a group of organic chemicals found in fruit which add body and structure to wine – the sensation of chewiness in young reds is due to tannin, it gives the wine body and longevity and means it stands up to strong food. Reds are often described as low or high in tannin – Beaujolais, for example, is typically low in tannin, while young Cabernet Sauvignon is often high.

Great care must be taken when crushing the grapes to release the right amount of tannin, colour and extract for the style of wine needed. Winemakers want to take the flavour from the skin, but not to squeeze the pips and stalks too much or a bitter flavour might leech out. For every red wine made, the type of crushing, gentle or otherwise, differs, and the length of time the juice spends sitting on the skins afterwards varies, and this all affects the final character of the wine. Expect crushed red grapes to sit on the skins for up to 30 days before the juice is run off.

Reds are not so sensitive to warm temperatures and indeed, some winemakers deliberately soak their reds on the skins (maceration) and ferment them at high temperatures in order to get more flavour and extract into the finished wine. Sometimes they push the floating skins and pulp down into the liquid, or pump it over on a regular basis to extract even more character.

The fermentation period can last for several days, perhaps with the temperature brought down a little over time. Sometimes the wine is pressed to collect yet more flavour, tannins and body, and then the wine is filtered off the solid matter and either stored in large containers, aged in oak, or bottled right away.

Rosé

What a shame rosé is so under-rated. An ice-cold glass of good rosé (or rosado, as the Spanish call it) is unbeatably refreshing on a hot summer's day and in my book there's no better match for a plate of jamón or seafood tapas. Still, pink wine lacks the structure and body of red and should be considered a fairly fragile style of wine that needs drinking up quickly after bottling. Rosé past its sell-by date is simply not appealing.

It needs to be made with great care - too many old, tired or oxidised rosés are lurking out there. Pink wine is usually made by crushing red grapes and leaving the juice to steep with the skins and solids for a short time (a matter of hours), then running off the lightly coloured juice and fermenting it.

Very occasionally a different method is used - a little red wine is blended with white wine to produce an in-between pink hue. This method is used in the Champagne region to make still rosé. Otherwise, rosé wine is made in the same way as white, with strict temperature controls (freshness is all) and especially quick bottling after fermentation.

And here are a few more technical notes for any budding winemakers:

Yeast

I love to think of wine as a living thing (after all, it does change over time and each bottle has its own unique character), but strictly speaking, the only important things living in the winery process are the millions of yeast that make the stuff. And yeast is killed off after converting sugar to alcohol (not such a bad way to go...).

Winemakers today have a choice of relying on wild yeast native to the vineyard and the air in the winery, or employing the use of cultivated yeast, which is created in laboratories. Some prefer the latter as they believe it leads to a more consistent and reliable fermentation; others think wild yeast gives a more authentic 'local' flavour to the wine. These people even say wild yeast adds a more interesting, individual, complex character to the wine.

Hygiene

Go into certain wineries these days and you will find a squeaky-clean environment, as sanitised as a hospital, with rows of sparkling stainless steel tanks, washed down concrete floors and walls, and plenty of workers ready with a hosepipe. Put it this way, it makes you feel self-conscious if you didn't shower that morning! Winemakers and their cellar-hands are acutely conscious of the need for hygiene these days, and work extremely hard to keep germs out of the winery. That's partly why they use stainless steel too - easy to keep clean. The old, smelly wineries of the past, where wine was much more susceptible to spoilage, are mainly gone, although a few still exist in poorer parts of the winemaking globe. That said, some highly rated winemakers still use 'open-top' fermenters and concrete tanks for convenience and because they favour the method, mainly for gutsy red wines. They do keep them scrupulously clean, however.

Feet

I have trodden grapes and had purple soles and toenails to show for it. That was during the port vintage in the Douro Valley, Portugal, and it was a surprisingly sensual experience to be up to my thighs in juice, stalks and pips. But few grapes are crushed this way any more. It's labour intensive and expensive, and wineries now have a vast range of sophisticated machines to do the job. There are gentle 'bag' presses which use a soft material to gradually, slowly, squash the fruit into giving up its juice while keeping harsh tannins at bay, and there are traditional basket presses, hand-controlled, which exert much more pressure, creating very rich tannic juice with plenty of extract. No, the feet can definitely take a rest.

Oak

The use of oak barrels is extremely important in adding extra layers of flavour and complexity to wine. A great deal of wine never sees the inside of a barrel, of course, and any simple, fresh, quaffing white or light, juicy red

has almost certainly not been 'oaked'. But some wines are fermented and aged in oak, while others are simply aged in barrels ('barriques' in French). Expect a creamy, rich, toasty character in oak-aged whites; a spicy, woody, vanilla-tinge in reds. More tannin is leeched out from the oak too. Oak barrels usually come from France, or America, where the wood gives a slightly more obvious, vanilla-and-sawdust character. They can be heavily toasted (charred inside) before use or more lightly 'seasoned' – it all affects the taste of the wine.

For a more subtle effect, winemakers can choose to age just a proportion of the finished wine – say, 30% of the Chardonnay is aged in oak, and blend it with 70% from a stainless steel tank to create the finished blend. Try to spot oaky characteristics in the wines you are about to taste. More on oak and the alternatives to oak barrels (chips, staves) in Stage Two.

Bottling

Another important consideration for a winemaker is whether to put his finished wine into bottle or

Sauvignon Blanc grapes arrive at a winery and are tipped into the containers that take them to the crusher. Time is of the essence to retain as much of the fruit's freshness as possible.

box, and whether to use a cork, a synthetic stopper or a screw-cap. Natural cork, made from bark, has been used for hundreds of years, and is still popular. However, it brings a problem in that a certain proportion (some say one in ten) is contaminated and spoils the taste of a wine. Plastic stoppers and screw-caps do not lead to these problems and some are predicting the increased use of screw-caps for quality wines in future.

There will be more discussion on this contentious issue in further parts of the book, but for now, take note of the different ways used to stopper your wine, and when you open a bottle with a natural cork, make sure it isn't tainted. A mushroomy smell, like damp cardboard, and a flat, musty flavour, are the give-away signs. These wines should be taken back to the shop – you should receive a replacement.

How to taste

There are still plenty of people who think tasting wine – taking time over it, mulling over its flavours, aromas and textures, perhaps even making notes – is a waste of time. They argue that wine is there only to be drunk, not fussed over. I think they are missing out. Of course there are moments when even wine professionals enjoy a drink without taking it seriously. But most people who have done a little wine tasting start to notice they enjoy wine a lot more, even on informal occasions. They simply get more pleasure out of each glassful.

Why? Well obviously, once you've learned something about wine, you are more likely to plump for one that suits you in the first place (or are more likely to avoid the duds!). And I think you are more likely to enjoy that extra-crisp flavour or that ripe, rounded fruitiness or that creamy touch of oak, however sub-consciously and briefly, if you have first discovered it when tasting wine more deliberately. Frankly, if you have never stopped to think when sipping wine, you will never know what it is in this wonderful liquid that really turns you on!

Apart from the alcohol that is. Sadly, some people drink wine just for the buzz, but if we simply wanted to get drunk, we might as well stick to plain vodka. No, the main reason wine is so adored is precisely because there is so much going on in every bottle. All those scents, undertones, hints and associations. The various textures, from silky-smooth, to tangy-tart, to rich and robust. A bit like art appreciation, the more we delve into wine tasting, the more satisfying and exciting it becomes.

By all means knock back a glass or three at a party, but for now, get started on some serious tasting. It doesn't mean turning into a wine bore, having to follow certain rules, or becoming horribly pompous – it simply means taking time to work out what YOU like best in wine. Proper wine tasting is fun. You can enjoy it on your own, but it can be wonderfully sociable if you get a group of friends together and turn it into a party with a theme – a bit like a book or bridge club, but more refreshing!

How to plan your tasting

Try to taste wine in the right environment. Choose a room that is reasonably light, so you can assess the colour of the wine, and create an atmosphere that is free of smells. The remnants of a spicy curry or a whiff of scented candles make it hard to 'nose' wine properly – and cigarette or cigar smoke is a serious obstacle. Open those windows! Keen wine buffs, by the way, don't wear perfume or aftershave when they are tasting.

Make sure you have a set of good, clean glasses. You will need at least two, preferably three or four, per person because it's helpful to pour several wines at once and compare their colour, texture and so on. Have a spitting place to hand (a jug, a vase, even the sink will do) for those who want to use it. Keep a notebook and pen handy for tasting notes – even if you don't plan to make them, you may want to write down the name of a particularly great wine.

Decide beforehand if the wines are to be tasted from uncovered bottles or 'blind' – if blind, you'll need to cover the labels with a bag fastened at the neck, or wrap the bottles in foil before getting underway (ask any guests to bring their bottles already wrapped up). The cork, and the outer metal or plastic capsule, sometimes state the name of the winery, so remove these too. Of course, this is very tricky if you are tasting on your own, but for more than one, I do recommend blind tasting, as it helps clear the mind of any preconceptions you might have. Blind tasting often turns up a surprise or two – the sceptic who never knew she liked Riesling, or the confirmed Francophile who rates the Californian Cabernet more highly! Give it a go. And consider giving marks (out of ten, or twenty) to each wine. It's not essential, but it is fun.

Lightly chill the whites, rosés, dry sherries and even perhaps the very softest, juiciest of reds – I've indicated exactly which bottles to chill in each tasting exercise which follows. Try to taste the lightest wine first through to the very richest. Whites should be sampled before reds, or the flavour of a rich red might overpower a weaker white that follows. You don't need to rinse your glass if a much more powerful wine comes next, but if in doubt, swill the glass round with water or pour a drop or two of the second wine, swirl it hard, then dump it, and after that take your tasting sample. As for your mouth – you should be able to taste up to four or five wines without needing to rinse, but have a jug of still, plain water and perhaps some dry crackers to hand in case you need to refresh your palate between mouthfuls.

Remember, no one is conclusively 'right' or 'wrong' in a wine tasting. If you reckon a wine is utterly delicious, while your friend thinks it stinks, then you are both right – you just have different palates, different tastes. It's great fun to debate the merits of wine, and it helps build up a reference library of descriptions when you compare tasting notes (you found 'fresh lemons' in the Viognier; he found 'stale mangoes'...). At the end of the day you will probably have slightly different views and that's just fine. We can't all like the same things in life!

Get tasting

Pour a small sample of wine into the glass. One-third is enough – don't fill up to the edge as it's useful to be able to swirl the liquid around to release the aroma. Take a long, hard look at the colour – it helps to hold the glass against a white surface (paper, wall, table napkin...). Is the wine clear or cloudy, bright or dull? How would you describe its colour? Look to see if it's viscous or thin. Swirl it around to get some indication of this. Heavy, slow-moving trails down the side of the glass – sometimes called 'legs' – indicate richness and possibly sweetness, while a thin, pale, watery liquid is likely to be a simple, drier wine.

Now swirl the wine vigorously in the glass and stick your nose in, taking a big sniff or series of smaller sniffs. Generally, we don't spend enough time thinking about the aroma of a wine, but it can give just as much sensory pleasure as the flavour. I have heard this 'sniffing' part of the wine tasting process described as similar to sexual foreplay, and we all know how important that is, so take your time. Think about the scents you find there – not only specific fruit aromas, but spices, flowers, leaves and grasses, chocolate, cream and coffee – let your imagination run riot.

Finally, it's time to taste the stuff! Take a big sip and let the wine flood over your tongue, moving it around your mouth and perhaps even pulling some air through it in a slurp. If this sounds rather visceral and unappealing, then that's because it probably is – it would certainly look and sound out of place at a vicar's tea party. But the point is to get as much of the wine's flavour released as possible. You can't do that by taking a delicate drop and simply swallowing it. (Oh, and don't expect to have white teeth by the end of a wine tasting either – purple fangs, black-rimmed lips and a splodge of red on the end of your chin are the usual results, if you are doing it properly!)

When you taste, think about the same fruit, spice and other flavours as you did with the aroma. Also think about acidity levels, oakiness, sweetness/dryness, tannin and, of course, general appeal. Is this a wine you want to drink again? Think, too, about the 'finish' – after you have spat out (or swallowed), assess the flavours again and decide how long they lingered, or what characteristic was left on the tongue. Some wines seem perfectly pleasant on first taste but leave a horrid, furry, tannic finish, while others end on a wonderfully well-balanced, satisfying, drawn-out note. Finally, it's fun to guess the cost of the wine and find out at the end of the tasting whether the price seemed right. Many an expensive bottle has been trounced by a cheaper one in a blind tasting!

A word on alcohol

If you are tasting, and carefully spitting out, just half-a-dozen wines, you don't need to worry about absorbing too much alcohol, even if you are driving, pregnant or simply trying to stay sober. The amount of booze absorbed through the mouth, and by swallowing saliva, is negligible (If you are tasting forty or fifty wines in one go, you may need to think again). But if you're swallowing the wine samples, it's well worth looking at the alcohol levels on each label and assessing just how much you are drinking over the course of a tasting. A light German Riesling might weigh in at just 8%, which doesn't give you much alcohol at all for just one tasting 'slurp', but a New World Shiraz is more likely to tip the scales at 14.5%. Just because you are approaching the subject more seriously than usual doesn't mean you won't get drunk! I prefer to spit out wine when tasting, remaining clear-headed throughout, and then enjoy a glass or two from my favourite bottle at the end of the session.

Glasses

Choose plain glasses for wine tasting – not coloured ones or cut-glass. This is because it pays to look at the wine's colour and texture, which is impossible with highly decorative glasses. Ideally, the glass should have a long stem, so you can keep your warm fingers away from the bowl holding the wine, and they should be thin, not chunky, to feel more delicate and appealing on the lips. Choose small or medium glasses, preferably with a fairly long bowl and slight incline at the lip, for whites, fizz, rosé and lighter fortified wines, and go for larger versions of the same for reds. Don't use tiny sherry schooners or champagne flutes for tasting as it is hard to swirl the liquid and aromas can be muted. Wash glasses in very hot water after use, using the absolute minimum of detergent, and dry with a clean linen towel.

Take note: describing wine

This book champions the idea of tasting, tasting, and more tasting as the best way to discover wine and reveal your individual preferences. So how do you make the most of your tasting sessions? First, concentrate. It's easy to get chatting about other things when you're looking at wine with friends, but try to switch off from the outside world and think hard about the aromas, flavours and textures of the wine in your mouth. That is why professional tasters, in theory at least, always try to taste in silence. You can gabble away about the wine and anything else you like after you've sampled each one!

Incidentally, some reckon it makes sense to taste in the late morning, when the tastebuds are supposed to be at their most acute. Most readers, though, will be tasting in the evening. That's fine, but don't eat strong or spicy food (or indeed, drink coffee or fruit juice) before sampling wine, as these will affect your ability to pick up subtle flavours.

The terminology of tasting

Tasting descriptions get a lot of bad press! It's hardly surprising - a wine bore can sound very pretentious if he (and it is usually a 'he', I'm afraid) rants on about 'finesse', 'complexity' or, horribly, 'naughty, cheeky little numbers' when describing wine at an inopportune moment. Who cares what he thinks if he wasn't asked, if the occasion is totally informal and if the wine is everyday party plonk? These people expose themselves to ridicule, and sound like gout-ridden old colonels from a by-gone era...

That said, realistic tasting notes that really mean something to you can be very useful when you're building up knowledge on the subject. Use terms that mean the most to you - not ones you've heard the wine bores use. For example, I could never get my head round the idea of a wine being 'masculine' or 'feminine', so I don't use those terms. I once heard a wine described as 'astute', which meant nothing to me. If a term sounds rubbish to you, don't use it! Come up with your own vocabulary.

Most wine drinkers today rely on fairly straightforward terminology to describe wine. Thus a tasting note such as 'rounded, perky little number with great finesse and oodles of charm' is considered old-fashioned and pointless by most drinkers, while 'fresh, lemony, light white with a floral aroma and a crisp, dry, yeasty finish' is a popular, modern style of tasting note. Thank goodness! The latter actually means something to

most of us, and conjures up a sense of what the wine tastes like much more clearly.

Think about associations with fresh fruits, as most wines taste of fruit (very rarely is it just 'grapes'). Some have dismissed this as the 'fruit-salad' school of wine writing, but it makes perfect sense to many - most wines *are* lemony or appley, or have blackcurrant, melon, strawberry or cranberry flavours in there somewhere. A few don't, especially very mature wines that have lost their primary fruit flavours and sunk (often beautifully) into more spicy, leathery, earthy notes, but most do. Try to think around the fruitiness - what about dried fruits (prunes, raisins and figs crop up regularly), peel, zest, stewed fruits, 'tart' fruit or 'sweetly ripe' fruit, and so on?

Think about fresh vegetables too - green peppers (capsicum), asparagus or cabbage (associations don't have to be nice!). And flowers (roses, honeysuckle, hawthorn blossom), herbs and grass. What about animal smells - the scent of sweat, of cat's pee, of mucky stables (yes, brace yourself!)? Or the natural smells of a damp forest floor, fresh warm earth, a sense of mineral spring water? Or even the artificial whiff of nail varnish remover, rubber tyres, cement, bright yellow banana chews, toffee popcorn?

Then there are associations with what I call store-cupboard food - items we smell and taste fairly regularly. I often find black pepper, chocolate, cloves, vanilla, cream, honey, tea-leaves and coffee crop up in the aromas and flavours of wines. Some of these (vanilla, spice, cream, butter, toast...) imply the wine has been fermented and/or aged in oak, while others imply maturity, or a particular grape variety. Use the information your senses give to enlighten you about the wine (especially in a blind tasting).

Marking

For some, a marking system is an essential 'short-hand' form of tasting note. They might mark wine out of 10, 20, perhaps even 100, or break the tasting down into sections on, say, colour, aroma, flavour, before adding all the marks up to find the overall total. If you're comfortable with this system, then go for it. It's certainly useful when trying to assess wine as a panel, because the average score of the group can be found for each bottle. This is fun if you want to discover the most and least popular bottles of the evening. But write a description down, too - a score of 14/20 without an accompanying tasting note doesn't mean a great deal several weeks down the line.

Chardonnay a world of contrasts

Not all Chardonnays are the same, by any means. The wines in this tasting are two contrasting styles made from the same grape. Use this taste test to compare how very different Chardonnays can be when they are made in hot or cool climates and using various winemaking techniques.

You are tasting...

Cool-climate Chardonnay
Try an example from Italy's Trentino area or Chablis in northern Burgundy. Ideally, pick a wine that says 'unoaked' or 'lightly oaked' on the label. Chill for 45 minutes, but make sure it's not too cold or the flavours will be muted.

Warm-climate Chardonnay
Pick an oaked example - the word 'oaked' will actually appear on either the front or back label - from a hotter region such as California, southeast Australia or South Africa's Stellenbosch area. Chill for 45 minutes, as before.

1 Cool-climate Chardonnay

APPEARANCE How would you describe this wine's colour? Is it a rich gold or a pale straw tint? Keep an eye out for any yellow or green highlights. Swirl the wine to assess its texture: does it look thin and dilute or rich and viscous?

AROMA Consider whether this wine smells fresh and appealing. Does it make your mouth water? Focus on its individual characteristics. Sometimes Chardonnay smells very fresh – greengages, lemons and other citrus fruits – indicating a cool climate and a crisp, tart wine. At other times it smells rich and tropical – peaches and pineapples – indicating heat and ripeness. Look out for other qualities too: Chardonnay sometimes seems creamy and vanilla-infused, slightly spicy or even toasty. This example may be clean, simple and uncluttered, if it is unoaked. What do you think?

FLAVOUR Is this wine fresh and attractive? Do you want to drink it or spit it out at once? Remember, a wine can taste quite different to the way it smells, so think about all those possible fruits afresh. Pineapples or peaches? Lemons or limes? Do any subtler flavours exist, such as a succulent mineral, almost salty quality or a richer spiciness, or do the fruit flavours seem ripe or tart? What about the acidity, and how dry is it? Texture deserves a moment, too. Is the wine thin or viscous, rich or light?

FINISH Does the wine end on a neutral note, short and disappointing, or leave lots of flavour in your mouth? Is it a simple yet refreshing wine, moreish and appealing, that you would like to drink? Or is it a heavy, rich wine that lingers on the palate, of which you can imagine tiring?

2 Warm-climate Chardonnay

APPEARANCE This wine was made in a hot region and aged in oak, so how does it appear next to the first wine? Is it deeper, darker and more golden? Assess its texture. Is it thinner and lighter, or thicker and weightier than the first?

AROMA What does this wine remind you of? Does the fruit cocktail of perfumes conjure up something specific, such as pineapple or mango? If you find one or two different fruits there, are they generally ripe and tropical or clean, tart and mouthwatering? Oak lends its own character to a wine, so can you smell the barrels? They might offer a spicy, vanilla-and-cloves character, or perhaps give a whiff of toast, roasted nuts or even coffee beans. Look out for cream and butter in warmer-climate Chardonnays, too.

FLAVOUR Think about the flavours, fruit or otherwise. Can you be more specific? Honeydew melons? Preserved lemons? Caramelised bananas? How does the acidity of this wine compare to the first? Is it drier or sweeter? Consider its texture, the rich fullness of the wine in the mouth. It will almost certainly be weightier than the cool-climate Chardonnay, as it is riper and oakier, which gives it more body and structure. Finally, assess the wine's more unusual qualities. Did you spot butter, spice, vanilla or toast in the flavour?

FINISH Warm-climate oaky Chardonnay typically lingers on the palate. So does this one measure up, or is it a weedy example? If it is full-bodied and flavoursome, do you like that? Would you want to drink much of it?

Merlot two takes on red

Just as the two Chardonnays in the previous tasting were alike in some ways, but utterly dissimilar in others, so it is with this pair of Merlots. Again, they are made from the same grape variety, but because other factors came into play, including very different climates, the end results form a stark contrast. As well as noting this, try to spot the typical Merlot character in both.

You are tasting...

Inexpensive European Merlot
Pick one from France, perhaps a cheaper label from Bordeaux, or one from the Trentino area of northern Italy. Don't go for serious, pricey, classed growth Bordeaux – the idea is to sample a relatively simple Merlot. Check on the back label that it is 100% Merlot, or ask the wine merchant.

Premium New World Merlot
Spend a little more and pick a big, powerful, oaky, warm-climate Merlot from one of the hotter New World spots – California, South Africa, Chile or Australia. The idea is to look at the contrast in styles, not to challenge the cheaper wine.

Taste both at room temperature.

1 Inexpensive European Merlot

APPEARANCE Have a good peer at the wine's colour, tipping the glass slightly so you can see the rim of the liquid – always a good way to assess a wine's style. How would you describe this colour? Think about the shade of red; is it bright and bluey-purple, or deeper and browner? Assess the wine's texture too – rich or thin?

AROMA Decide whether the first impression leaves you keen to sample the wine or not. Focus on the individual smells. Merlot should always have a generously fruity aroma, immediately appealing, fresh and inviting. Does this wine have that quality? Think about exactly how ripe the fruit seems to be by its aroma – bags of squashy, juicy red berries might jump out at you, or there may be a more stalky, green, unripe note. And is there a spicy note of oak, or does this smell like a fairly simple, fruity wine?

FLAVOUR Think about the fruit flavours in more detail. Strawberries, plums or cherries – which ones can you find here? Is it a full-bodied, powerful flavour, or a light, refreshing one? The texture is important, so think about whether the wine is thin or viscous, soft and smooth or tannic and chewy. What about any interesting hints of spice or chocolate, cream or coffee? Maybe a green stalky note is present in the flavour too – if so, is it appealing or not? Try to assess any oaky quality to the wine. Is this a well-balanced wine, overall?

FINISH Sum up the length of flavour – does it disappear immediately, or does it linger on? Is this wine complex on the finish, with interesting flavours and undertones creeping in at the end, or is it simply refreshing and fruity? Do you like it?

2 Premium New World Merlot

APPEARANCE Tip your glass again and compare the colour at the very edge of the liquid with the previous wine. Is it darker, richer or a different shade of red? And is the texture the same, or does this wine seem richer, thicker, or lighter, thinner than number one?

AROMA This wine will probably smell richer, more heavily aromatic, but decide for yourself. Look for the signs of oak ageing – spices such as clove, nutmeg or cinnamon, a coffee/chocolate/vanilla quality, or just the basic scent of new oak, like freshly planed wood. Is this attractive or not? Are the fruits the same? – look out for the specific fruit aromas here. The fruit might seem riper and richer too. Perhaps a slightly baked, raisin character, or a sweetness may spring to mind.

FLAVOUR Think about the fruity flavours again – how ripe do they seem, compared to the previous wine? Is there more sweetness this time? And what about that oak – do the wood flavours seep through more on this wine than on the previous one? It should be richer, bigger and weightier in texture than the previous one, but is it well-balanced? Do the acidity, sweetness and tannin levels go well together, or is one element overpowering? Does the richer style work?

FINISH It's important that the tannins are not too dominant on the finish of this wine, and that the oak is not overpowering. Check the balance again and note whether the finish is lingering and attractive. Decide if you like it and if you would want to drink much of it. Or is it a 'show-off' wine that isn't particularly refreshing and moreish?

White varieties a trio

For the third tasting, the aim is not to compare wines made from the same variety, but to look at three whites made from three highly individual grapes, all coming from Europe, and from areas relatively close to each other (compared with other, far-flung regions of the globe). This tasting should highlight the major taste differences between the three white grapes in our 'Big Six': Chardonnay, Sauvignon Blanc and Riesling.

You are tasting...

German Riesling
Pick a dry or off-dry style. The word 'trocken' on the label will help you choose – it means dry. 'Kabinett' means the least ripe style, so plump for that too, or you may get the impression of sweetness. Go for a fairly young wine – from the same year as the other two preferably. Make sure the bottle actually says Riesling – no cheap imitations in the form of Liebfraumilch!

European Sauvignon Blanc
Inexpensive, young and simple. Try a Sauvignon de Touraine from the Loire Valley in France, or a Sauvignon that says Vin de Pays du Jardin de la France (a 'country' wine from across the Loire Valley). If you can't find one, buy a Sancerre or Pouilly Fumé from the Loire, or buy a Sauvignon Blanc from Italy, Spain or Hungary instead.

Medium-bodied French Chardonnay
Pick a Chardonnay that is well-balanced, buttery but not over-oaky. A Chablis (from northern Burgundy) would be perfect, or a Vin de Pays d'Oc Chardonnay from the deep South. Again, pick a fairly recent vintage and an inexpensive bottle.

Taste all the wines lightly chilled.

1 German Riesling

2 European Sauvignon Blanc

APPEARANCE Take a good look at how pale this wine is. It probably has no rich golden glint at all, but a light straw colour – you may even spot hints of green in it, but it looks pretty watery. Give the wine a swirl and note if the texture is thin or rich.

AROMA Riesling is often described as 'appley' in aroma (which sort of apples – green, yellow, ripe, crunchy?), and there's usually some crisp citrus fruit there too. Another scent to look out for is a floral one – a trace of blossom on the perfume. Don't expect it to leap out of the glass, however. This should be a light, pretty aroma, one that conjures up spring meadows and freshly chopped orchard fruit.

FLAVOUR I want my Riesling to be very fresh, clean and mouthwatering, with good crisp acidity. Does yours taste like that? Are those orchard fruits there again, or is the citrus note more prominent? Most important after that essential freshness is the balance between the high acidity, the ripe fruitiness and the dryness/sweetness. Is there harmony in this wine? Does its light touch work for you, or do you find yourself wanting a richer white wine?

FINISH Riesling should leave you feeling refreshed, and your palate clean. You should be begging for more – this is an ideal aperitif wine and should make your mouth water for another sip. That's only if you had a good example though – a poor Riesling might be dull, bland and insipid. What do you think? Is the finish dry enough? Imagine, too, which light foods would complement it – salads, fish and seafood?

APPEARANCE Compare and contrast the look of the two wines so far. Does the Sauvignon Blanc have a slightly richer colour, a greener hue? Look at the texture, too, as always.

AROMA The scent of Sauvignon Blanc is very distinctive. Watch out for gooseberry and lemon, with subtler nuances that might include grapefruit, freshly chopped grass and even a hint of tom cat! There's a fresh, crisp immediacy to the aroma, one that draws you in and makes your mouth water, and it smells as though it will be a dry, refreshing wine. Or that's the idea anyway. Does your wine smell like this? Is it actually pungent, or just nicely aromatic?

FLAVOUR Young, cooler climate Sauvignon Blanc should be tremendously quaffable, slipping down easily with a dry, fresh and pure quality. Does this describe your wine? Try to identify the flavours and work out if they are the same ones you spotted on the nose. It's important to think about the acidity levels – these wines can be too sharp and tart, so is the acidity well-balanced here? Think, too, about how thin or rich the wine is.

FINISH Does this wine perform its main function, which is to be a dry, refreshing, wake-up-the-tastebuds type of white? Or is it disappointingly short and dull after tasting? You should be left with quite a zingy, clean flavour in your mouth, and some of that gooseberry and lemon, plus a subtle mineral hint, should linger a little, too. Would you describe this wine as complex or fairly simple?

3 Medium-bodied French Chardonnay

APPEARANCE We've looked at Chardonnay already, and seen that it can be rich gold or a much paler yellow. See how this one fits in to the Chardonnay colour spectrum, and compare it with the first two wines, as it should certainly be a little deeper in colour. Compare the texture too - it could well look like richer, thicker liquid.

AROMA It's fascinating to discover different fruit aromas in different white wines. The Riesling should have conjured up apples, the Sauvignon gooseberries and lemons, so what do you notice here? Think of more tropical fruit, such as peaches and pineapples, and ripe oranges or tangerines. Are any of these fruits present in the scent? And can you detect any oakiness? - perhaps this wine smells slightly buttery, biscuity or toasty.

FLAVOUR The main objective here is to compare the taste of the European Chardonnay with the flavours of the European Riesling and Sauvignon. There are those different fruit flavours again, and perhaps the hints of oak - look out for vanilla on the flavour. The texture is interesting, as it is almost certainly a lot richer and more rounded than the previous two wines. But make up your own mind - is this a richer wine? And do you find it more appealing?

FINISH Does the flavour linger long after the tasting? Can you pick up richer nuances on the finish, perhaps a creaminess or a slight nuttiness? Try to imagine this wine as an aperitif, like the other two. It probably doesn't seem so appropriate. Chardonnay is more often used to match with food, so which dishes do you think would work well here, and are they the same as the Riesling food matches?

What did you think?

You've just sampled wines made from the three best-known white grape varieties in the world. Do you think this trio deserves its extraordinary popularity? How do they differ from one another? Which one would you want to try again - instinctively, which is your favourite? Another useful experiment is to try matching each wine to a particular occasion - which one best suits a hot summer's day in the garden, which one would fuel a party, which one goes with roast chicken, and so on. Overall, was the quality acceptable? Work out whether you thought each wine was worth the money, too.

Ripe reds getting warmer

Red wines from newer parts of the winemaking world tend to be richer, riper, juicier and more 'fruit-forward' than their counterparts in Europe. But all New World reds do not taste the same. Of course, the grape variety used plays a large part in the flavour profile. Here are three reds, each from 'hot spots', all made from very individual grapes. Note the ripeness they all have in common, then it's time to spot the differences...

You are tasting...

New World Pinot Noir
Pinot should never be grown in very hot climates – it just doesn't suit the grape – but it is made in increasing quantities in the slightly cooler, but still sunny, areas of some newer winemaking countries. Find a young one from New Zealand, California or Chile for this tasting.

Warm-climate Merlot
Go for a wine labelled Merlot from South Africa, Chile, Argentina or California. OK, Sicily is in Europe, but its modern, newly overhauled wineries produce New World lookalike wines, so a Sicilian Merlot will do here, too!

New World Cabernet Sauvignon
Pick one from a warm place – from Australia, the Barossa Valley or Hunter Valley, or from California's Napa Valley, or from Chile or South Africa. Make sure it is a similar age and price to the other two wines.

Taste all these wines at room temperature.

1 New World Pinot Noir

APPEARANCE Your wine should have a bright red-purple colour, and look fresh and appealing. Pinot Noir turns browner with age, but this is a young wine and it shouldn't have matured very much yet. This wine may look a little lighter and 'thinner' in texture than the next two.

AROMA I want a very appealing, fruity scent from my Pinot Noir – above all, a fresh strawberry and cherry aroma, one that really leaps out of the glass. That bright primary fruit should be the most obvious characteristic, but do look out for hints of chocolate, cream, perhaps a slight leafiness too. And is there any light spiciness that might indicate the wine has aged in oak?

FLAVOUR The texture of Pinot Noir is famous, and much loved for its smooth, silky softness. The wine may taste tangy and succulent as well. But notice the lack of hard tannins and the fact that it seems so rounded and mellow. Is this easy-drinking wine, compared to the other two? Expect that bright red berry fruit again, especially strawberry, and perhaps some subtle hints of nuttiness, toast and cream.

FINISH Soft and smooth again, this wine should leave relatively little trace of tannin, although that fresh fruit should linger nicely and there should be a tangy acidity about the finish that leaves you wanting more. That's the idea anyway – this wine may not measure up, however! Assess the wine for these qualities and decide whether you would class it as light, medium or full-bodied.

2 Warm-climate Merlot

APPEARANCE I hope for a very bright, deep garnet colour in my Merlot, especially if it has come from a warmer climate, so I would certainly check for that. Assess the richness of the colour and the texture of the wine by swirling it around the glass.

AROMA Merlot should sing out with fruity perfume – lots of ripe, juicy strawberries, plums and other red berries. Try to pin down exactly what you find here, and look for other nuances, too – spice, cream, chocolate... Or is this a Merlot with a greener, more stalky, under-ripe streak? It shouldn't be, but you never know...

FLAVOUR Bags of red berry fruit, and a ripe, juicy flavour are a must here, but is that what you find? The body and structure will be interesting. Some Merlots are medium-bodied, not too powerful, but as this one comes from a hotter climate and may have been aged in oak, it might be chunkier and richer than usual. Would you describe it as full-bodied, and does it seem quite tannic, or is it smooth? It could be either... Are there traces of oak ageing here?

FINISH That structure and body will be easy to assess on the finish, as you are left either with a smooth, rounded flavour, or a chewier, heavier one. Which foods would you match with this wine? Merlot is extremely trendy right now – can you see what the fuss is about? Did you like it more or less than the Pinot Noir?

3 New World Cabernet Sauvignon

APPEARANCE Cabernet has a very rich, deep colour, so check out your wine and see if you spot this. Young Cabernet Sauvignon should look more bluey-purple, while older wines have a redder, brickish tint. Spot the density of the colour, and try to rate the thickness of the liquid.

AROMA The hallmark of fine Cabernet is its ripe blackcurrant aroma – is this evident in your wine? From a New World region, where the winemakers usually major on very fruity styles, it should be a marked cassis aroma. Look out for other signs, too – an oak-aged Cabernet will have a spicier note, perhaps with toasted nuts, vanilla, cinnamon and cloves, while some Cabernets have a more minty, leafy note.

FLAVOUR The distinctive cassis should be there, along with other fruits – blackberry, plum and others, perhaps. Again, try to spot any more unusual characteristics – signs of oak ageing. Sometimes tasters find 'lead pencil' in Cabernet, or cedarwood, or a peppermint or eucalyptus hint – what about you? Then think carefully about texture. Is this a very rich example of Cabernet? Can you taste the tannins – a slightly furry, chewy texture – and are they in balance with the wine?

FINISH Tannins show through on the finish, so re-think the level in this wine after spitting it out. Is the flavour lingering or short? Do you get more of that lovely Cabernet cassis coming through? Think about oakiness, sweetness and acidity levels too. Does this wine need more time to soften and mellow, to lose its hard edges? Would you drink it on its own or with food and, if so, which dishes? Is this more full-bodied than the previous two wines?

What did you think?

Three of our most famous red grapes – three very contrasting styles of red wine, although they each come from new, relatively warm wine-producing areas. Spotting the various fruit flavours, and the more subtle undertones typical of Pinot Noir, Merlot and Cabernet Sauvignon is well worthwhile, as is a look at tannin and structure in each wine. Which did you favour most highly, or is it simply a case of contrasting wines that would suit different occasions or different dishes?

Pink & white summer refreshers

Forget boring, bland white wines - some whites have very extrovert personalities and can be quite distinctive in a tasting. Here are three white wines which should get your adjectives flowing. They are made either from Riesling or Sauvignon Blanc, in parts of the world well known for top-quality examples of these grapes. The fourth wine provides a good introduction to quality rosé.

You are tasting...

Riesling from Alsace, France
The Alsace region of eastern France is well known for its aromatic, premium white wines. Its Rieslings are among the best made anywhere. You can expect a richer, more full-bodied wine than the German one we tasted earlier on...

Australian Riesling
... but not as richly fruity as an Aussie Riesling. Try to find one made in the Clare or Eden Valleys of South Australia, where the wines have a very characteristic limey tang when young.

New Zealand Sauvignon Blanc
The Kiwis have wowed the world with vibrant, pungent Sauvignon Blancs. Go for the Marlborough region, on the South Island - Sauvignons made here are most typical of the New Zealand style.

French Rosé, made from Merlot
Rosé from the Bordeaux region is usually made from Merlot, and the grape should be named on the label. Go for a very recent vintage. Rosé from another country, made from Merlot, would do here.

Chill all these wines well before tasting.

1 Alsace Riesling

APPEARANCE Would you describe this wine as gold, green or pale straw? Try to pinpoint the colour accurately, comparing it with the whites we have had in previous tastings. Alsace Riesling is often a little 'thicker' in texture than German Riesling, so give it a swirl and decide if you think it looks rich or thin.

AROMA Remember the German Riesling (see page 35) that was so appley? Do you find the same character here, or is this wine more citrussy, peachy, or are there other fruits coming through on the aroma? Some people find a certain steeliness, like a mineral quality, almost flinty, to this style of wine. Do you? Or are there traces of honey, petrol, lanolin – all used to describe Riesling sometimes? Notice the lack of oak on the aroma – Rieslings are hardly ever aged in oak.

FLAVOUR Is this wine light and refreshing, rich and satisfying, or somewhere in between? Is the acidity in good balance, or is it too tart or too flabby and lacking in bite? What about the sweetness/dryness levels – sometimes Alsace whites can be surprisingly sweet. And which fruit flavours and more exotic notes can you spot on this wine? Importantly, do you like it?

FINISH Another good moment to assess acidity and sweetness levels is on the finish. Overall, is this a well-balanced wine, and does it seem vibrant and youthful or soft and mature? Think about whether the flavour lingered and if this was a mouthwatering aperitif white, or a richer wine that makes you want to try it with fish, salad or chicken.

2 Australian Riesling

APPEARANCE Compare and contrast the look of this wine with that of the previous one. Is it a deeper green, or gold, or paler than the Riesling from Alsace? Does it seem thinner or richer in weight?

AROMA This style of Riesling, from relatively warm Australian vineyards, should be packed with fruity flavour. Don't expect the delicacy of German Riesling – although this is not a powerful, pungent wine, it will have a more obvious aroma. But of what? I often discover citrus – lime and satsuma – in these wines, but maybe you won't... Look out for some honey and beeswax, perhaps a light smokey note, or a dab of marmalade, too.

FLAVOUR The flavours really should reflect the aroma – lots of fresh, tangy, juicy fruit, probably citrus. Also a palate cleansing acidity, which should, incidentally, be in balance with that ripe fruit. Look out for more subtle notes in the wine and decide if the overall style works – not too sour, not too sweet, not too tart.

FINISH Any young Riesling should wake up the taste buds and leave a refreshing taste in the mouth. Does this one? Is the acidity balanced, or is it out of kilter? Note the lack of oak, and decide if this wine needs drinking up now, or if it should be left to mellow a little over time. Compare it with the previous wine.

3 New Zealand Sauvignon Blanc

APPEARANCE There may be some greenish hints in the wine, but otherwise it is probably quite pale - Sauvignon Blanc usually is. Check out the texture too - it may not be quite as thin and watery as some light dry whites.

AROMA There should be lots to comment on here - gooseberries, lemons, passionfruit, grass and fresh herbs. Perhaps some green asparagus, tomato leaf and even sweat or tom cat - a more animal note. Let yourself get carried away describing this wine, as Marlborough Sauvignon Blanc is one of the most aromatic whites around. And if there isn't a fresh and obvious scent coming from the wine then, sadly, you have got a poor example. Assuming there is, however, do you like the smell, or do you find it a bit overpowering?

FLAVOUR That racy, lively gooseberry fruit should burst onto the tastebuds too. Check that the acidity is correct - clean and crisp, but not too tart. If there's a grassy streak to the wine, make sure it doesn't come across as too stalky and under-ripe. Is this wine totally dry or is there a hint of sweetness? And do you find such an extrovert wine delicious or rather over-the-top? Would you want to drink more than one small glassful of it?

FINISH Again, look for a tangy succulence, but not too much - your mouth might water but hopefully you won't be wincing in pain! Did the flavour carry through to the very end of the mouthful, or did it simply fall off and end rather abruptly? How did the finish of this wine compare to that of the Rieslings?

4 Rosé made from Merlot

APPEARANCE The colour of rosé wine should be one of its great attractions, so it's worth paying a bit of attention to this wine's appearance. Some rosés are deep cerise, almost like a light red, while others are the palest blossom pink. Where does this fit into the spectrum? Is it orangey-pink or purpley-pink? Is it clear and bright, and does the liquid look thin and dilute or richer than that?

AROMA Ditto - the aroma is particularly important, as rosés should be very fresh and appealing, conjuring up summer berries merely with their scent. A dull aroma means the rosé will taste insipid or is tiring. Look out for red berries from the Merlot grape - perhaps cranberries, rosehips or wild strawberries. And maybe a creamy quality to the smell too.

FLAVOUR Don't expect a great deal of powerful flavour from a pink wine, not as much as on a red Merlot, anyway, but do expect freshness and crispness. The acidity should be tangy and quite obvious without being tart. Does this rosé measure up? Would you describe it as refreshing and attractive, or has its bloom faded? And assess the sweetness level - is it slightly sugary or dry?

FINISH That sweetness/dryness balance and the fresh acidity should be easy to look at on the finish, too. Check on the wine's tanginess again, and whether those red berry flavours keep going long after swallowing. Don't anticipate a strong finish, but look out for a delightful, palate-cleansing end to a good rosé.

What did you think?

This tasting probably inspired some strong feelings - you either like each of these wines a lot, or you really don't! Which ones did it for you, and why? Which particular characteristics are your favourites - the tangy acidity, the fresh vibrant fruit flavours or the lack of oak? Or are you yearning for a rich, buttery Chardonnay after all? And did the rosé surprise you? Select one wine from the four above to match with each of the following dishes: mild chicken curry; fresh grilled fish; cheese quiche; cold meats and salad. There are no 'correct' answers here, it's just an interesting way of looking at the wines!

Cabernet & co duelling duos

This tasting could be described as slightly more sophisticated - or more tricky - than the ones we've had so far. The four wines here are made from, or are based on, the same grape variety - Cabernet Sauvignon, undoubtedly one of the world's greatest. One wine is 100% Cabernet, but three are blends. In each of these three, the Cabernet forms a duo with a different grape variety. See how that changes the flavours.

You are tasting...

Pure, 100% Cabernet Sauvignon
If you can find one, Chilean Cab would be the best, as it sings out with varietal character. Bulgarian or Southern French Cabernet are good bets too. Go for a good quality, fairly pricey bottle, to keep the cost in line with the other three.

Bordeaux blend
Buy a wine from the Médoc region of Bordeaux, which will be predominantly Cabernet, blended with Merlot (and perhaps other varieties, too). Try to find a bottle that states the proportions on the back label. Keep prices similar for these wines.

Australian Cabernet-Shiraz blend
These are widely available, a New World classic double-act. Buy one from any region, or a cross-regional blend from, say, southeast Australia.

Italian Cabernet-Sangiovese blend
This may be harder to track down, but Tuscany produces quite a few of these blends today. The back label will probably tell you which grapes are in the blend.

Taste all four wines at room temperature.

1 Pure Cabernet Sauvignon

APPEARANCE We've already discussed the typical deep, dense colour of Cabernet, so check out this wine for that hue. Think about ways to describe it – purple, mahogany, rich garnet – try to expand your vinous vocabulary!

AROMA You should be getting used to that distinctive blackcurrant/cassis aroma by now, so give this wine a good sniff and see if it's there, or if other fruits are apparent. Assess the wine for other notes – the cedarwood, mint, chocolate or spice that might be in this particular wine, and any oaky traits. This is your 'control', 100% Cabernet, so take good note of it and contrast it with the other three.

FLAVOUR Again, pin down the character of true Cabernet. Blackcurrant, maybe blackberry, those more subtle notes of spice and oak. Think about the 'mouthfeel' of the wine and the element of tannin. Is it well-balanced? Is there a freshness and a quality of pure primary fruit? Is it one-dimensional or satisfying? Do you like it – or can you imagine that the addition of another variety might add more interest?

FINISH Another chance to decide if you like Cabernet on its own, or if you think it would be better in a blend with another grape variety. Does it have a mouthfilling, satisfying, balanced finish? Cabernet is sometimes accused of being too austere and tannic, so do you think a juicier blending partner would help – or do you like this wine just as it is?

2 Bordeaux blend

APPEARANCE Hold the wine up to the light and compare it with number one. Is the colour darker, denser, lighter or thinner? Look at the edge of the liquid to decide if it is brick-red or a more purpley-red.

AROMA Is the typical Cabernet blackcurrant still there – or does it seem as though different fruits have joined the scent? Red berries, perhaps, from the characteristic flavour of Merlot. Or maybe not, if the Cabernet is still dominant. Check it out, and decide if you think this has a more interesting, complex and appealing aroma than that of straight Cabernet.

FLAVOUR Again, consider the main differences between these flavours and those of the pure Cabernet. Is the blackcurrant still evident? Or has it turned into a more general 'summer berries' taste? It is often claimed that Merlot is added to flesh out the tough Cabernet with more generous, plump fruit – would you say this wine shows that? And what about tannin levels, oak influence and general texture? Does this combination of grapes add up to a more 'rounded', well-balanced, complex wine, and do you like it more than the previous one?

FINISH Good Bordeaux should be very well-balanced indeed – showing no over-riding tannins, but a good, firm structure. The tannins should be fine, the oak subtle and enhancing, the fruit ripe but not too jammy. It's a tall order – does the finish of this wine measure up? How does it compare to the previous sample?

3 Australian Cabernet-Shiraz blend

APPEARANCE Keep the other two wines in their glasses for comparison. You might just find this wine looks darker and richer in colour than the others. Hold it up to the light, tip to see the rim of liquid and describe!

AROMA Australian wines tend to be ripe and fruity, with a fairly obvious rich aroma of black fruit or black fruit gums. The Shiraz may have added a spicy note – can you spot pepper, cloves or nutmeg here? And sometimes I find a toffee or treacle note in Cabernet-Shiraz blends – you may do, too. Overall, how is the aroma of this wine different from the previous two? Is it jammier, riper?

FLAVOUR Look for the influence of Shiraz – a spicy note, some toffee or pepper, perhaps even a bit of gaminess. How do the fruit flavours seem – particularly compared to the other wines. Are there red fruits or black ones here? How are the tannin levels and the oak? How do the elements of Cabernet and Shiraz get along together – do the flavours blend well and complement each other, or are they out of harmony? Are there two separate parts to the flavour, or is there a pleasant melding of the grapes' personalities?

FINISH It's interesting to compare the finish of a hot climate Cab-Shiraz with a Bordeaux Cab-Merlot. Are the tannins giving the same structure or is one more powerful, chewy and robust than the other? Is the ripe fruit of the Aussie wine more or less lingering than the previous samples? Are you left with a more spicy finish? (There will be more on Shiraz later in the book, see page 80.)

4 Italian Cabernet-Sangiovese blend

APPEARANCE By now you have a framework of reference for the Cabernet blends – where does this wine fit into the palette of colours? Is it darker or lighter, brighter red or more brown?

AROMA Sangiovese is the main grape behind Chianti and is often tasted almost entirely on its own, where the predominant aroma is strawberry with hints of tobacco and tea (more on this variety on page 59). So what happens to Cabernet when it is blended with Sangiovese? Does the strawberry or the blackcurrant aroma win out, and which more unusual notes emerge? Is this a bigger, more powerful wine than the other three, or not?

FLAVOUR Again, look for the merging of flavours between the two components – do they seem to complement each other and make a winning flavour combination? What about tannin and acidity levels – Sangiovese can have quite a tangy edge, so is it present now?

FINISH Do you like this wine? Does the combination of Cabernet and Sangiovese work for you? As you spit or swallow the final red, consider its complexity, length of flavour, and which characteristics are left lingering on the palate the longest. Try to spot any creamy oak, or chewy tannins as well. The Italians are very keen on food and wine matching, so which dish do you think might work best here?

What did you think?

Although all contain Cabernet Sauvignon, the four wines should reveal how blends create different styles. True, they come from far-flung regions of the world, and the various climates, as well as other factors, affect them too, but this is a useful way to get used to the idea of blends, compared with 100% varietal wines. You may have a favourite among these four, and you may have strong views on value for money, too, as they are not especially cheap wines. Try to match them with specific dishes too - particularly red meats, strong cheeses, rich game or spicy recipes.

Buyer's guide

Now that you've embarked on some serious tasting, it will be useful to brush up on your wine-buying skills. Try not to lunge for the first bottle you see – take a bit more time to choose wine carefully. Here are some tips that should help, and more follow in later stages of the book.

Good advice: Supermarkets

Lots of people still grab any old bottle in the supermarket, particularly when there's a special offer on, and then wonder why they are disappointed.

Wine shops usually report an amazing response to special offers – the minute a wine has money knocked off, or becomes part of a BOGOF deal (Buy One, Get One Free), it is snapped up. This is fine, if you know you like that particular wine, but it is risky if you haven't got a clue what it's like. Look at the label and check the vintage – don't buy an old, tired bottle of a style that is supposed to be enjoyed when it is young, such as light dry whites, rosés, cheaper bubbly, soft, easy-drinking reds and dry pale sherries.

However, if you know what you like and you've got the storage space, it's clearly worth stocking up when that wine is on a 'special'. Bulk-buy if you're planning a party, when you'll want lots of wine at a great price. The bigger retailers have the edge here – good prices, even better deals, fast turnover of inexpensive, drink-'em-up-quick wines, and the convenience of large car parks!

Some merchants offer the last few bottles of any stock as 'bin-ends', and put them on high discount. It's worth taking a look at these wines. Sometimes the offers indicate a real bargain – a serious wine that is just at the end of its run. But watch out for light, aromatic dry whites, rosés or frivolous sparklers being offered as 'bin-ends' – they may be tired and past-it, and they may have sat under hot shop lights for too long. Only buy wines you know are young and fresh, or richer reds that can take some hanging around without deterioration.

Labels: Own-brand

Should you buy own-label brands from stores (Eezy-Bye's Chablis), or go for the smaller producer (Little Valley Chardonnay), or the big, glitzy, famous labels? Firstly, a canny wine consumer never gives up on the cheaper end of the market. OK, avoid the absolute rock-bottom, but as your tastes grow more sophisticated, don't entirely forget about those inexpensive bottles. Remember, you never know when you might find something wonderful at a low price, or something that is perfectly palatable for everyday drinking. Keep your eyes (and tastebuds) open and receptive!

However, one of the reasons mass-market wine producers are so powerful is that too many consumers are apprehensive about buying obscure labels. Avoid getting stuck in a rut, and never be scared to try something different.

Shop alternatives: Mail order/internet

Wine is a heavy, difficult commodity to lug about. Try taking a case home on the bus! Recently there has been a dramatic rise in the number of mail order and internet services offering a wide selection of wines, and it may make sense to use these. The delivery charges tend to be small and the wines can be high quality, if you shop around enough. Do use a reputable, well-established company though, and avoid the very cheapest, 'special offer', pre-mixed case – some mail order/internet companies use these to off-load bland, boring bottles. And bear in mind that by purchasing this way, you lose some of the pleasures of browsing for wine, handling those bottles yourself, examining the labels and chatting to the manager.

Things can always go wrong with home deliveries, too. However, I tested several well-known mail order companies recently, ordering a case of wine from each, and I was pleasantly surprised by how efficient and fast the service actually was. Use this way of buying wine when it suits your purposes, but perhaps not exclusively.

Drinker's guide

Wine tasting has a serious purpose - to help you enjoy drinking the stuff even more! Once you've put the spittoon away for the weekend, here's how to get the most out of wine when you're matching it with food, storing and serving it. More on these themes in later stages of the book.

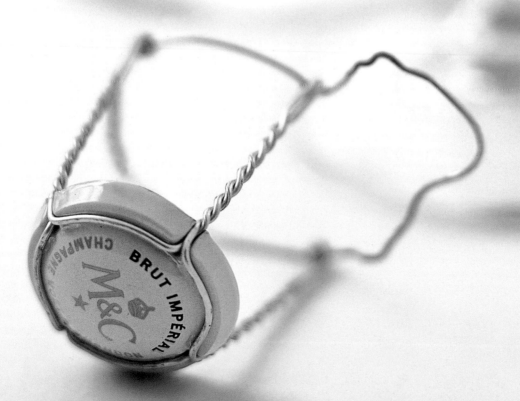

Food matching: Simple, everyday...

Are there any important rules about wine and food matching? None that can't be broken! If you like a particular wine with a particular dish, then that's great – no one should tell you you're wrong. Nowadays anything goes in food and wine pairing – some red wines have been found to suit certain fish recipes, for example – but it is worth bearing in mind that a good balance between food and wine usually works best. Match like with like, and don't let either the food or the drink element overpower the other. So try dry, refreshing whites (Riesling, Sauvignon Blanc, Muscadet, basic Chenin Blanc) with light party snacks, salads, fish, seafood and delicate chicken dishes. Richer whites (Chardonnay, Semillon, Viognier) suit roast chicken, fish or chicken in creamy sauces and luxury seafood like lobster or crab. Soft, easy-drinking reds go with simple tomato pasta sauces, pizzas, cold ham and vegetarian bakes, while more powerful reds work better with red meat, peppery sausages and full-flavoured cheeses. Elegant sparkling wine is delicious with the lightest and most subtle of party canapés; but match powerful port with hard, sharp cheeses, chocolate or fruitcake.

Storage: Opened bottles

Although a great deal is written about 'cellaring' wine, or 'laying it down', the truth is the vast majority of bottles is cracked open within a few days, and many within a few hours. If you are keeping wine for such a short time, then you don't need to bother with storing it in a cool, dark spot like a cellar, or laying it on its side to stop the cork drying out. Your wine will not spoil in two days.

That said, keep the bottles away from direct sunlight, hot radiators or other heat, including the oven. Extremes of temperature, particularly heat, will quickly affect wine. The best place to store wine in the short-term is in a cool room, in its original cardboard box. You can keep whites and rosés in the fridge for a few days, but it's marginally better to store them at room temperature and chill them for a couple of hours before opening, as very low temperatures can deaden the flavours and aromas slightly.

Remember, there is nothing worse than being offered a glass of a once-splendid wine that comes from an old, dusty, oxidised bottle that was opened three months ago (or possibly three years ago, in the case of Christmas sherry!). Wine deteriorates rapidly after opening, because the air gets to it, and so it must be enjoyed when fresh or tipped into the stew... or down the sink!

As a rule of thumb, light table wines (white, red or rosé) and dry pale sherries need finishing within two or three days of opening. Re-seal them with the cork or screw-cap between servings, and store them in the fridge or in a dark spot. Richer reds (and perhaps the very richest whites, ones with good acidity, ripe fruit and full-bodied flavours) last four days or so, while ports, rich sherries and dessert wines last for seven to ten days. I know many who keep their port much longer than that, but I think it deteriorates quite obviously after ten days.

Fizz can only be kept for more than a few hours if you use a special seal, and even then it loses some sparkle. There are various products that claim to keep still wines for longer by creating a vacuum at the top of the bottle, or by spraying a layer of protective gas over the surface of the wine. They work reasonably well if you can be bothered with them. But why not buy wine in half bottles if you won't get through a standard-sized one in a few days?

Serving: Chilling and breathing

Chilling certain wines brings out the crisp tang and makes them appear more refreshing. Dry, medium and sweet whites, rosés, dry and sweet pale sherries, and sparkling wines (even red) really must be chilled. Try chilling light, juicy reds for a short time too, and even tawny ports. Serve other wines at room temperature, but no warmer.

There are a lot of myths about opening wine to let it aerate or 'breathe' before serving. The thinking is that the wine will soften and mellow out if it is exposed to air. For some, this has become a ritual – several hours before a dinner party, they open the wine and let it stand so it is ready for drinking later on. The fact is, they are probably wasting their time. Most wine produced today is supposed to be drunk as soon as the bottle is uncorked. In the past, highly tannic, tough reds were the norm.. But now winemakers generally produce more rounded, easy-drinking, fruity reds, and most of these wines are delicious when young and newly opened.

If you are sure you want to aerate your red, pour the whole contents of the bottle into a clean glass decanter, where the air can really get to it. This is a nice way of presenting the wine too, and if the wine has any sediment, you can separate it and throw it away.

stage 2

It's time to take things a bit further, with a look at more fascinating grape varieties and a closer examination of the subject of blending. Plus, we pop the cork on some sparkling wine. There are also six more tasting exercises that build on the knowledge acquired in stage one. By now, you should be beginning to get a sense of which wines work best for you. Keep going and become more wine wise!

The second team

Now for a second helping of grapes! We've already taken a close look at the six most famous varieties of all, and each can be wonderful in their own way. It's a good foundation of knowledge, but it doesn't pay to get stuck in a rut, tasting only Chardonnay, Cabernet and other very well known varieties. Becoming a wine expert is about trying all sorts of flavours and styles, and recognising the vast range of tastes, smells and textures that comes from a host of different grape vines. Use that knowledge to build a further framework of reference by comparing and contrasting more wines with one another.

So here are another six grape varieties, all fairly well respected, generally popular and widely grown. It's also useful at this point to start thinking more about blends. Most of the wines discussed in Stage One were made with just one grape and it's easy to imagine most bottles contain just that. In reality, a high proportion of the wine we buy is a blend of varieties, and that ranges from cheap basic bottles to top-notch labels such as the famous blends of Cabernet and Merlot, or Semillon and Sauvignon Blanc.

Sometimes a blend comes about simply because a winemaker wants to use cheaper grapes and pad them out with a more expensive and better quality partner. Sometimes it is purely for aesthetic reasons - fruity, soft, aromatic grape A complements tougher, more tannic, but longer lasting grape B. A few argue that the best blends are more complex, more compelling, have more depth and character. The truth is, there are great wines made from single varieties, and there are poor ones. Ditto for blends!

Semillon

I mentioned blends in the introduction to this selection of grapes, and blends are especially relevant when it comes to Semillon. Most of us drink this variety as part of a duo, usually paired with Chardonnay for a reliable Australian white, easy-drinking, soft and fruity, or with Sauvignon Blanc to make the great whites of Bordeaux, both dry and sweet.

But don't pass up the chance to try Semillon in its single-varietal glory. Usually this will be an Australian wine. The Aussies are good at Semillon, making fine examples in the Hunter Valley in New South Wales, Clare Valley and the Barossa in South Australia. These are distinctive wines. They start life a little like Sauvignon Blanc, grassy with fresh citrus juice (some are oaked and vanilla-laced, others are left bare and can seem simple in the early stages), but with age they mellow and fatten splendidly, taking on the quite different characteristics of honey, beeswax, smoke and toast. So it can be quite a surprise if you squirrel away your Semillon and crack it open several years later. Save these mature, full-bodied wines to match with fish or chicken in creamy, buttery sauces.

Back to the idea of blends. Over in Western Australia, around the Margaret River area, Semillon is partnered with Sauvignon Blanc to make some very sophisticated dry whites. In this neck of the woods the winemakers look to Bordeaux as a role model, so it is hardly surprising that they copied the classic white Bordeaux blend. In France, this can be a stunning meeting of grapes, as the richer, fatter, creamier Semillon is complemented beautifully by the sharper, more crisply fruity Sauvignon Blanc.

The Graves region of Bordeaux makes the best wines, some of which are richly oaked and age well over a long period, acquiring honeyed, nutty notes and losing the lemon freshness of youth. Then there's Sauternes and its neighbour Barsac, where magnificent sweet and luscious wines are made from our happily married pair. There will be more on these dessert wines and how they are made in Stage Three.

There isn't an awful lot of Semillon made elsewhere in the world, although look out for rare examples of rich, dry wines from America's Washington State and South Africa.

Pinot Gris/Grigio

A grape variety with two very public faces, and very different styles. The best-known incarnation of this grape is Pinot Grigio, the Italian white that is currently enjoying enormous popularity as an easy-going, everyday 'quaffing' wine. I must own up and say that I can't quite see what all the fuss is about. Most Pinot Grigio tastes exactly like the ocean of other cheap Italian white wines – reasonably clean and fresh, but neutral and uninspiring. I would rather 'quaff' Sauvignon Blanc or Riesling any day.

The best examples have a bit more character – usually fresh citrus and pear, even a hint of almond oil if you are lucky. It's certainly worth buying a superior (i.e. more expensive) Pinot Grigio from a reputable producer rather than bog-standard, bargain bottles. Most of it comes from the cooler northern vineyards of Italy, particularly Trentino and Alto-Adige.

So far, so uninspiring. But then there's Pinot Gris from Alsace – same grape, but a quite different creature. In Alsace, Pinot Gris (usually called Tokay-Pinot Gris, though it has nothing to do with Hungarian Tokaji) can be beautifully rich and exotic, unoaked, but with a full-bodied texture and spicy, smoky notes underlying peach and apple. It seems to bear absolutely no relation to its weedier Italian counterpart. Poor examples can be a bit sugary and lacking in crisp acidity, but buy a good Alsace TPG and you are tasting one of the world's top whites, and a brilliant match for rich fatty food (confit de canard, poultry pâtés, cheesy quiches and other egg dishes).

Loads of whites made from Pinot Gris are now pouring out of the newer wine countries – a lot of them are disappointing: off-dry, flabby and non-descript. But there are some decent examples, with a good weight and zest and concentration of spicy apple and pear flavour. Most of the successful wines come from Oregon and New Zealand.

Viognier

Pinot Gris may be fashionable right now, but Viognier has long been seen as rather chic. Perhaps that's partly because it is made in such tiny quantities in the area where it is most prized – the northern Rhône Valley in France. Here two small areas, Condrieu and Château-Grillet, make incredibly intense, aromatic whites from this grape. The perfume is redolent of late summer – all peaches and apricots, with some white blossom and honeysuckle thrown in the mix. Indeed, this grape can make such scented wine that small amounts are sometimes blended with Syrah in the reds of the Northern Rhône to give them more aroma.

The flavour should be concentrated, rich and peachy, too, and in the Northern Rhône it often is. But then prices here are high – often ridiculously so – while elsewhere in France Viognier can be a serious letdown. This is not a particularly easy grape to grow – the vine flowers unevenly and doesn't always ripen well. It needs to ripen properly to develop those lovely scents and flavours, and crops must be small if the grapes are to produce intensely flavoured wine.

These are the reasons why so much dilute and downright boring Viognier exists. It takes a skilled winemaker to pick the grapes at exactly the right moment and it means us paying a little more to get a good wine made from low-yielding vines. A few fine (and lots of reasonable) Viogniers are made in the South of France (vins de pays d'Oc), and one or two Australian and Californian bottlings are testament to the fact that it can be made well outside France, but there are some disappointing wines out there too. Not bad, you understand, but dull.

It's a shame, simply because Viognier can be so exciting. If you get a good bottle, it is one of the few whites that really works well with creamy curries (especially fruity ones), and with chicken in creamy, buttery sauces. It's that full on; that much of a character.

Shiraz/Syrah

A grape variety with two names – I bet there are lots of drinkers who are blissfully unaware that these are one and the same vine. The French call this grape Syrah and make some of their top full-bodied reds from it. The Australians call it Shiraz and, er, make some of their top, full-bodied reds from it. Elsewhere, from South Africa to Italy to New Zealand, they choose whichever name they fancy and try their best!

It is certainly a variety that is taken more seriously now than it used to be. The Australians in particular thought of it as a 'workhorse' for decades and were happy to churn out bog-standard, rough and ready wines labelled 'Dry Red' made from Shiraz. Then, in the 1970s and '80s, they realised that their ancient vineyards of huge, low-yielding Shiraz vines could make the intensely concentrated, powerful, blackcurrant wines that became some of the most distinctive Australian reds of all. The country's most famous wine, Penfold's Grange, is made from Shiraz. Enough said.

The same 'wow' factor is certainly there when you come across the majestic, dark, glowering reds of another hot vineyard area – France's Northern Rhône. Wines like Côte-Rôtie, Crozes-Hermitage, Cornas and St-Joseph are rich, spicy, peppery monsters when young but more mellow and approachable with time. Expect some blackcurrant and blackberry, but these wines do not major on fresh fruit flavours. Instead, there are tar, liquorice, toffee, herbs, leather and oak nuances in most wines. Somehow, they seem more elegant than Australian examples, graceful despite their power.

What about the Southern Rhône? Syrah is rarely seen on its own here, but it is one of the grapes used in the extraordinary mix of varieties that creates Châteauneuf-du-Pape, and it crops up in the blend for Gigondas, Lirac, Vacqueyras and others too. Basic Côtes du Rhône reds may contain a lot of Syrah, but they tend to be a bit jammy and simple, so trade up to Côtes du Rhône-Villages for better quality and value for money.

Syrah makes more reliable, ripe and rounded reds in the South of France (Languedoc) and you might come across one or two interesting examples from Italy. In the New World of wine countries, New Zealand is making elegant versions, more in line with the Rhône style than the Aussie. South Africa, America and Argentina are other sources of some exciting Syrah/Shiraz.

Sangiovese

Sangiovese is not terribly well known. Or, rather, it's not as well known as the wine it makes, which is Chianti from Tuscany in central Italy. It deserves to be more celebrated, as Chianti is a perennial favourite and recently quality seems to have got a lot better, making Tuscany one of the world's most exciting red wine regions once more.

Sangiovese (the name means Jove's blood) is widely planted in Italy, sometimes under different names, but it is as the main component in Tuscan reds that it reaches its apogee. That word component – yes, we're talking blends again. Sangiovese may form the mainstay of the wine, but it has Canaiolo and other grapes in the blend too. It also plays a major role in another well-respected Tuscan red, Vino Nobile di Montepulciano. To make the other celebrated Tuscan red, Brunello di Montalcino, it is used on its own.

Look out for the high acidity when you taste a wine made mostly or entirely from Sangiovese. This sour-cherryish 'bite' on the finish is more appealing than it sounds and makes the wine extremely food-friendly, as it seems to cut through the fattiness of meats and cheeses. But the wine isn't exactly light, as this might imply. Good Tuscan red should be medium-bodied, with plenty of intense, red-berry aroma and flavour, and Sangiovese often brings notes of fresh tobacco, tealeaf and herbs into play too.

In the modern era of winemaking, it has often been blended successfully with Cabernet Sauvignon to make so-called 'Super-Tuscan' reds, which fall outside the normal regulations of the region. Look out for Sangiovese-Cabernet blends from up-and-coming Tuscan appellations like Carmignano, Pomino and the coastal Maremma area – they can be deeply impressive.

All that aside, a word of warning. Sangiovese suffers in cooler years, and if the grapes are high yielding you could well end up with a glass of sour, astringent red. A generation ago, most of the Chianti sold in those notorious straw flasks tasted like that. Today standards are much higher, but buy a very cheap bottle in your local trattoria and you still risk everything!

Not much Sangiovese is grown elsewhere in the world, although a few palatable bottles have appeared from Argentina and California. Winemakers in America and the Antipodes are currently keen on all things Italian, so expect more in the future.

Tempranillo

What Sangiovese is to Italy, so Tempranillo is to Spain. In other words, this is its top red grape. The one that, above all others, defines the flavours of a typical Spanish red, if such a thing exists in a country that makes so many varied styles of wine. For most people, Spanish red still equals Rioja, and Tempranillo is the great grape of Rioja.

Rioja is an area in the north of the country where the reds are typically aged in American (not French) oak, and released as mature, mellow, soft wines ready for drinking. It's a popular myth that red Rioja is robust and full-bodied. It's not – there's plenty of ripe strawberry and vanilla character, sure, but the smoothness gives away the long ageing process that both *reserva* and *gran reserva* wines have undergone. *Reservas* must age for at least three years, including one in cask; *gran reservas* undergo a minimum of five years ageing, including at least two in cask.

Nowadays the rules are there for breaking, and several wineries in the region use French oak (less vanilla, more subtle spice) and Cabernet Sauvignon as a blending partner, while others release very young unoaked wines (*joven*) or ones that have had a shorter time in barrel (*crianza*). But Tempranillo tastes as good as ever, and its hold over the rest of Spain, where it goes under several different names, is as strong as ever. Branch out and try it as Tinto Fino from the Ribera del Duero region for a change – the wines can be remarkably intense, savoury and satisfying. Do what the Spanish invariably do, and use it to wash down red meat, preferably lamb, which makes a magnificent partner.

Nowadays, winemakers in different parts of the globe are keen to try out Tempranillo. Most New World countries have one or two examples. There are a few made in Argentina, which are rich, ripe and smooth, and I've even come across Tempranillo in New Zealand. The trademark strawberry flavour should be there.

The vineyard

In Stage One, we looked at different types of vineyard and the concept of *terroir* – the elements that make up a particular plot of land and its influence on a vine. The climate, the soil, the gradient of the slope – all these factors and many more, as we have seen, determine the taste of the wine in your glass.

But is *terroir* an exclusively European idea? Do the growers working in newer parts of the winemaking globe own very different vineyards from those working in traditional areas? It's easy to picture a stereotypical French vineyard as small, wild and natural, compared with an Australian one which, you might imagine, is huge, uniform, with regimented pruned vines stretching across a vast tract of land. But that isn't the reality.

Australia might have some huge vineyards – particularly in areas turning out vast crops of grapes such as Riverina – but it does have plenty of small ones, too. Visit Tasmania, or the Yarra Valley in Victoria, and you can see lots of small plots of vines, often owned by one family.

Not all of them are stripped bare of weeds and grass – some of them look quite untamed and natural. The same goes for certain vineyards in California, New Zealand, Chile and South Africa. In France, there are vast areas covered in large vineyards, for example in the deep south of the country, stretching out as far as the eye can see. Other regions, such as Bordeaux and Burgundy, contain much smaller patches of vines.

In short, wine drinkers imagine a more stark contrast between the so-called 'Old World' winelands (Europe), and the 'New' (everywhere else) than actually exists. Take the attitude towards *terroir*. This was originally a French concept – look at the way the French usually put place names on a label instead of grape varieties. The belief is that it is not a 'Pinot Noir' in the bottle, it is a 'Gevrey-Chambertin' – an expression, in the form of red wine, not of a grape, but of the very essence of that particular part in Burgundy. Historically, this has happened elsewhere in European winemaking – the Germans, Italian and Spanish put great store in a wine's origins.

The stereotypical 'New World' winemaker could not give a fig for the place where the wine is made. To his (or her) mind, the winemaker and the grapes used are far more important factors, and the vineyard is just a big patch of land. This caricature of an Aussie or Californian producer would suggest that any half-competent winemaker can fashion a palatable wine from a truckload of grapes, no matter where they come from.

But the stereotype no longer holds true. New World winemakers have come round to the idea of *terroir*. For evidence of this, refer to the labels once more. Top bottlings from New World countries nowadays often place great emphasis on the region or even the single vineyard where the grapes were sourced. The winemakers there have embraced the idea that the place where the grapes are grown has a great deal to do with the quality and character of the wine.

Likewise, winemakers in Europe – even in the traditional parts of France – are not putting quite so much emphasis on *terroir*. They recognise that the role of the winemaker, the grape variety and the equipment in the winery are all important factors too. A modern label from the South of France might shout in big letters the grape used, but not say much at all about the area beyond 'vin de pays d'Oc'.

The two sides are coming together. As you work through the various tastings in this book, try to think about *terroir* and the role of the vineyard, as well as the job of the winemaker and the character of particular vines. As the tastings get more sophisticated in this and the final stages of the book, you might start to spot the influence of *terroir* much more.

Global warming

Another factor bringing traditional and newer vineyard areas closer together is global warming. As I write from my study in Devon, England, I can report that English vineyards basked in the sun this year (2003). It has been one of the warmest summers on record. The first reports of the 2003 vintage are glowing – even taking into account the usual hyperbole of the PR gurus!

In some European wine-producing areas, the extreme heat combined with drought to shrivel and cook the grapes. But in England the warm sun meant diseases such as mildew were kept at bay, and they ripened effortlessly and earlier than usual. Even the reds are said to be highly promising from this vintage. I haven't tasted them yet, but I have high hopes. Global warming is very bad news on many levels, but for grape growers in marginal climates, it can mean much better crops – and better wines.

Many wine critics believe the best wines of all are made in 'marginal' climates - those where the conditions are cool to the point of being tenuous. Although cooler climates can lead to poor crops in bad years, when the sun shines and the rain holds off at the right moments, the result is potentially more elegant and complex wines than those made in scorching hot conditions. Areas such as Marlborough on New Zealand's South Island, France's Loire Valley, Tasmania, Oregon, Chile's Casablanca Valley are all cooler spots than usual and winemakers start to worry when the weather is especially cold and damp. But given a good, warm, dry year in these places, a full ripeness combines with a fresh acidity and purity to give a bit more balance, freshness and complexity to the wines.

Problems arise, however, when the area is too marginal - i.e. right on the edge of viable conditions for grape growing. This sometimes happens when a region is enjoying huge success and prosperity, and growers start to plant beyond the best sites. Some think this is happening in Marlborough, where all the top spots are already filled with vines, and much colder plots of land

Old vines develop wonderfully gnarled, thick trunks but the fruit quality doesn't usually deteriorate, even for vineyards over 100 years old. Instead, as the crops get smaller, the juice concentrates.

are being dug over and planted. This can certainly be bad news when the frosts start to roll in while the vines are flowering in the spring.

'Vieilles vignes' - a taste of maturity

A word about maturity. In the vineyard, great age is definitely a good thing. Vines are no good for wine grapes at all in the first couple of years, and it is only after four or five that they begin to produce decent fruit. It can take a lot longer than that for the quality of the grapes to peak. Older vineyards are much more desirable than very young, immature ones.

Why? Well, older vines tend to produce smaller crops of more highly flavoured grapes. The concentration of acids, fruit flavours, tannins and so on is greater. Not such good news for the grape grower, who gets a smaller yield from his vineyard, but great for wine tasters. In actual fact, many growers place a premium on grapes from much older vineyards and charge more for their fruit. Then the winemaker might charge more for the wine – so we end up paying! Which is fine, as long as the quality is higher (you can't guarantee it).

How old is old? Think of it on similar terms to man's average life span. Vineyards are considered mature at between ten to twenty years, and wines made from vines thirty, forty, fifty or sixty years old are quite common. Occasionally the vines are more than one hundred years old, as is the case in some Australian Shiraz vineyards.

When the French produce a wine from a notably old vineyard, they often put the words *vieilles vignes* on the label. Do look out for this, and try to spot the characteristics of mature fruit, whether they be extra concentration of flavour and varietal character, a noticeable thickness of texture, or higher tannin content. Remember, though, that these traits may simply be due to the grape variety used and/or the work done in the winery.

The future's bright, the future's organic

An awful lot of myths exist about organic wine. Some people think it's made from different grapes than ordinary wine (actually, some believe it's not made from grapes at all, but from turnip tops or dandelions), and others think they can drink as much as they like without getting a hangover (at least, they do until they try it once...). And some think organic is defined by what happens in the winery – the banning of certain chemicals in the winemaking process. In truth, the only really important difference between organic wine and non-organic is what goes on in the vineyard.

Or, rather, what does NOT go on. Organic wine is quite simply made from organic grapes, ones which have been grown, ripened and harvested without the use of fungicides, pesticides, herbicides or artificial fertilisers. The vineyard must have been free of such chemicals for a set period of time before the grapes were grown there (usually three years) and a regulatory body, such as the Soil Association, grants the organic status after a thorough inspection.

Natural methods can be used. These include planting specially chosen 'weeds' between the rows of vines to balance the soils or add more nutrients, and introducing natural predators to vineyards to keep pests down (such as a wasp that eats the bugs that ruin leaves). The advantages to both the soil and the microclimate are obvious. You only have to walk through an organic vineyard to notice the healthy, natural life around you – grasses and other plants underfoot, worms and insects abound, the skies full of birds – so it is definitely in the long-term interest of the grape grower not to strip his soil and ruin it for short-term gain.

That said, it isn't always easy to grow grapes organically. In areas where the damp and humidity create rot and disease, some spraying may be hard to avoid. Although many growers have converted to organic viticulture in recent years (and many have always been organic), others have not. Interestingly, a significant number of growers around the world have opted to go only 'so far' – limiting the amount of chemicals they use, resorting to them only when strictly necessary. They may not describe their wines as 'organic', but they often boast about their chemical cutbacks somewhere on the label, and why not?

Unfortunately, organic viticulture is more costly and labour-intensive than using chemicals, and it follows, of course, that organic wine can be a little more expensive to buy (around 10% on average, as a good guesstimate). It doesn't mean, I'm afraid, that organic wine is always more tasty. Its fans argue that it produces better quality grapes, truer to varietal character and truer to the natural *terroir*. But most blind tastings prove that there are great organic wines and there are some absolute stinkers. And many more in between.

But for the sake of the land, it is certainly worth going organic. You may even find that if you are allergic to traces of certain chemicals (and especially to sulphur, which is added to organic wine in much smaller amounts than to non-organic), then organic gives you fewer headaches. One thing's for sure, however. You will still get a hangover if you drink too much alcohol!

Organic vineyards, showing an abundance of wild flowers growing between the rows of vines. In non-organic vineyards these would not be allowed to survive, and would be destroyed with chemicals.

In the winery

Sparkling wine

How do the bubbles get into sparkling wine? While it's fun to imagine someone pumping washing-up liquid into vast tanks of dry white, that wouldn't lead to very refined flavours and aromas! Although the very crudest method does resort to something like a soda-stream pump, thankfully the most common ways of producing fizz are far more sophisticated.

And for sophisticated, read 'expensive', of course. Anything that takes a long time in the winery, and is labour-intensive, is bound to push up the price of your wine. And we all know how expensive Champagne is. That's partly because there is fierce demand for the wines from this one small region of France, and partly because of high marketing and advertising costs among the competitive Champagne houses. But it is, to be fair on the Champenois for once, mainly because their highly traditional winery techniques are so laborious.

This is how the Champagne method works (it was once called the *méthode Champenoise*, and now is known as the *méthode traditionnelle*): The grapes (Chardonnay, Pinot Noir and Pinot Meunier) are pressed very lightly to give a clear juice. A thin, light, dry white wine is produced from it. This is bottled with the addition of a little yeast and sugar so that it begins to ferment again, and the top is stoppered so that the CO_2 gas produced by the fermentation cannot escape. The 'sparkle' is trapped inside the bottle. The wine is left to age in the bottle, sitting on the yeast sediment, which gives it some extra creamy, yeasty flavour. Eventually, through a painstaking series of gentle twists over a long period of time, the bottle is moved to an upside-down position in the cellar, so that the sediment moves to the neck of the bottle, which is then frozen. The plug of solid icy sediment is removed and the bottle topped up with sweetened wine, which determines more precisely the 'house style' of that particular Champagne. The bottle is then sealed with the distinctive mushroom-shaped cork and wire cage.

Bottles of Champagne in a traditional 'cave' (cellar). They are turned by hand gradually over a long period until upside-down, so the sediment falls into the neck and can be removed more easily.

This method is not only used in Champagne, but throughout the world for premium sparkling wine. Cava is made by the same method, but using different, Spanish grape varieties. The word Champagne can only be used in the Champagne region around Reims and Epernay in France, and the three grape varieties Chardonnay, Pinot Noir and Pinot Meunier are the only ones permitted in Champagne. The first two are widely used in other sparkling wines too. *Blanc de blancs* refers to a Champagne (or sparkler) which is made using only white grapes (Chardonnay in Champagne). *Blanc de noirs* refers to one made using black grapes alone. The former tends to be creamy, elegant, fresh tasting, while the latter is richer, firmer and more aromatic. Brut means dry and demi-sec means sweet.

Although it is generally thought that this method makes the best sparkling wines, there are other, cheaper ways of getting bubbles into bottles. The transfer method involves second fermentation in the bottle as before, but the fiddly business of removing the sediment is avoided by emptying all the bottles into a tank under pressure and filtering it all in one go. The sugar solution is added here and the wine is rebottled. The wine still picks up some yeasty character from ageing on lees, although the result tends to be a little less elegant, and the bubbles a little more coarse and large.

Then there's the tank method, also known as the bulk or Charmat method. These wines do not undergo a second fermentation in bottle. It happens in large tanks, to which yeast and sugar are added. The popular sweet Italian fizz Asti is made this way. Another method worth noting is the wonderfully simple and ancient French tradition of trapping a wine in bottle while still undergoing its first fermentation. This leads to sweet, frothy, sometimes slightly cloudy wine and is used around southern France. The light but refreshing Clairette de Die is made in this way.

More and more countries are getting in on quality sparkling wines. The producers need a source of fairly cool-climate fruit to make that thin, acidic base wine, so sparklers made in hot areas tend to be inferior. Still, most countries can find a cooler vineyard or two. Even the Australians make decent bubblies from grapes grown in the Yarra Valley, Adelaide Hills or Tasmania – cooler places that give the required type of fruit. Look out for sparkling wine from New Zealand's Marlborough region, California's cooler vineyards and England's handful of accomplished sparkling producers for a taste of the best fizz outside France. And look for a category of French fizz called *crémant*, which indicates a bubbly made to strict regulations in the Champagne method, but outside the Champagne region.

A word on rules

I'm convinced that some of the jargon surrounding wine laws is utterly off-putting to most wine drinkers. You see phrases such as *appellation contrôlée* or *Qualitätswein mit Prädikat* on a wine label, and it's baffling. Many of these words refer to the laws governing wine production in a certain part of the world, and let you know which quality category the wine falls into.

The French system starts at the bottom with *vin de table* – the most basic category of table wine, which can come from anywhere in the country. *Vin de pays* is a category invented about thirty years ago, which has stricter regulations attached to its production. It translates as 'country wine' and each *vin de pays* comes from a specific geographical source – hence Vin de Pays d'Oc from the Languedoc, or Vin de Pays des Côtes de Gascogne from the Gascony region. *Appellation contrôlée*, or AC wines, are much more strictly controlled, and are supposed to represent the top quality level of French wines. There are regulations defining vineyard area, grape varieties, yields, alcohol levels and sometimes winery practices.

In Italy, Portugal and Spain, terms such as DO, DOC, DOCG and DOCa follow the same lines – these are the top tiers of regulated wines. Basic table wines are known, respectively, as *vino da tavola*, *vinho de mesa*, *vino de mesa*. In Germany, where the system is extremely complicated, the top wines are labelled *Qualitätswein bestimmter Anbaugebiete* (QbA) or QmP (as above), with a further definition of the dryness/ripeness level of the wine inside the bottle.

Don't make the mistake of assuming that all the best wines automatically fall into the defined top categories, however. There will always be some disappointing AC wines, as there will be duds labelled DOC or DOCG. And some more basic wines can be surprisingly good.

An interesting post-script to this: in the modern winemaking era, some European producers have rebelled against the hard and fast rules governing the top categories of wine. Why should they make wine under strict controls just to gain an AC or DOC status,

they ask? Some of them have proved that by breaking the rules, they make refreshingly different, high quality wines, which fall into 'lesser' categories. One example is Super-Tuscan red; often impressive, innovative blends that miss out on being labelled DOC (the top tier in Italy) because of their use of forbidden grapes. In France, some talented producers opt for a *vin de pays* status for their wines instead of AC, so they are freer to make their bottles the way they want. The best of the mavericks are to be applauded for breaking away from tradition and creating exciting new wines.

More on oak

We've looked at the widespread use of oak barrels, and the effect that fermenting and ageing the liquid in wood has on a finished wine. But not all 'oak-aged' wine is kept in barrels (*barriques*, in French). Just as there are cheaper ways to make sparkling wine than the *méthode traditionnelle*, so there are shortcuts to achieving that oaky character in a wine. Barrels are very expensive and need to be overhauled, repaired or replaced fairly regularly. No wonder many producers look at the alternatives.

The most obvious alternative, widely used for inexpensive modern wines, is oak chips. Instead of putting the wine into those costly barrels, it is kept in a tank and a bundle of small oak pieces is added. The effect is rather like dunking a tea bag into hot water. The oaky flavour leaks out into the wine and the wood is removed when the influence is deemed enough. The effect is more crude than that from barrels, however. The subtlety and fine enhancement that can be achieved by barrel ageing is replaced by a fairly obvious woody flavour. Fine, in its place, for cheap and cheerful wines, but no good for top quality *cuvées*, which deserve more refined oak treatment. Another alternative is the use of oak staves. Staves normally make up barrels, of course, but it is cheaper to put a few in a tank of wine instead. Again, the result is a little cruder. Experienced wine tasters can often tell which wines have been oaked using barrels, and which using staves or chips. These methods are all legal. Use of artificial oak essence, however, is not, although that doesn't mean it is never used!

Wine stored in oak barrels rests in a winery cellar. The oak is not only there to contain the liquid – it also adds some flavours and aromas, often a spicy, toasty character, to the finished bottle.

Stylish whites a new quartet

It's time to taste other white varieties, after getting to know the three main white grapes in Stage One. Here you can compare four new styles of white, not only with the now-familiar Chardonnay, Sauvignon Blanc and Riesling, but alongside each other. By the end of this tasting exercise, you should have a fair idea of your preferred taste in dry white wine.

You are tasting...

Italian Pinot Grigio
This is a cheap and cheerful style of dry white. Pinot Grigio usually comes from the north of Italy. Make sure you buy a young, sprightly example, as older wines may taste tired.

Tokay-Pinot Gris from Alsace
A more serious wine, made from the same variety. It costs more, but it doesn't matter if the wine is older as it keeps much better. In Alsace, the grape appears on the label, so finding the right wine should be easy.

Australian Semillon
Choose a medium-priced bottle that is a year or two in age. The best areas to go for are the Hunter Valley, New South Wales, Barossa or Clare Valleys in South Australia. (A Semillon from South Africa or South America will do instead.)

Southern French Viognier
Not Condrieu, which costs a lot more than the other bottles. Look for a wine labelled Viognier from the Languedoc (Vin de Pays d'Oc) or choose a Viognier from a newer wine region (Australia, South America, South Africa, California).

Taste all these wines chilled.

1 Italian Pinot Grigio

APPEARANCE Pinot Grigio from cooler climates usually has a very pale, watery appearance, possibly slightly green. It may look a little thin too, when you swirl the liquid around in the glass. Is this neutral, dilute appearance a turn-off?

AROMA Ideally, the wine should have a subtle, summery and rather mouthwatering aroma. Light scents of crisp lemon and pears should waft up from the glass. There may be a note of almond too. But poor Pinot Grigio smells of very little at all. Is the scent discernible, fresh and inviting, or is it a wash-out?

FLAVOUR In my view, the most important quality Pinot Grigio should have is a fresh, crisp flavour. A certain citrus fruitiness should be there, and a superior example will not be too thin or watery, but will even have a note of creaminess. So how does your wine measure up? Does it taste young and vivacious, or is it tired and dull? Also think about the acidity – in an unbalanced wine it might be too flat or too sharp. Is anything else going here, such as a slight prickle of CO_2 gas, indicating youth?

FINISH In a good example, there will be a refreshing, cleansing, wake-up-the-tastebuds finish. Expect this wine to have a fresh, tangy 'lift' at the end, rather than a disappointing tail-off! Were you left with lots of pure citrus or orchard fruit flavours?

2 Tokay-Pinot Gris from Alsace

APPEARANCE There should be some striking differences between this wine and the previous one, despite the use of the same grape – and it starts with the look of this wine. Note how much richer and more golden this wine is, and how it looks a little thicker and weightier when you swirl it in the glass.

AROMA Nothing like the Italian Pinot Grigio again, or let's hope not, anyway. The Alsace wine should be more aromatic, with subtle and rather exotic undertones of spice, smoke, cream, peach and apricot. Nothing too overt, but forget the crisp, simple citrus fruit of the first wine. You are looking for more complexity here.

FLAVOUR Some examples of Alsace Pinot Gris, it must be said, are disappointingly flabby – in other words, they lack fresh acidity. So a good example will have a crisp, zingy streak to balance out that weighty fruit. Then look for signs of richness, of orange fruit (not just oranges, but peaches, apricots...), and those quiet hints of cake spice and smoke. Expect a richer texture than you got with the Pinot Grigio.

FINISH If the wine is one-dimensional and flat on the finish, then you have a dud on your hands. Tokay-Pinot Gris should leave you with a lingering richness of flavour. Check the acidity again – is it in balance? Would this make a good food wine, do you think? Do you think this wine is more complex and interesting than the previous one? Did you have more to say about it?

3 Australian Semillon

APPEARANCE A bright, rather yellowish wine should greet you – clear and quite vivid in its colour, especially compared to the very pale, watery hue of the first wine. Check for richness – I'd expect a medium-bodied white here, but find out before going on.

AROMA Young Semillon has a grassy aroma – it can smell similar to Sauvignon Blanc in that respect. Intriguingly, more mature Semillons take on a much richer, toasty scent, with ripe limey depths. Try to work out if yours is showing these (welcome) signs of age yet. Sometimes I pick up a slight smokiness with Semillon, a honeyed quality, creaminess, even a touch of spice. Your wine may be more simple than that – but it's worth looking out for all of these traits.

FLAVOUR Texture is interesting here too. Younger Semillons taste thinner, more grassy, tart and refreshing than older wines, which start to develop that famous beeswax and cream note, with hints of toast and spice. Assess your wine on this basis. Do you think Semillon has an overtly fruity flavour, and if so, which fruits can you spot here?

FINISH Again, balance is everything – the wine should leave a refreshing tang in the mouth, and at least a little of that toasty, creamy, beeswax note should linger. Do you think this wine would be a good light party 'quaffer' or a bottle to match with food? Give your reasons.

4 Southern French Viognier

APPEARANCE Another wine that should be bright and golden – more towards golden-green than anything, but a 'normal' yellow glow is important. The richness of the liquid will tell you a lot – if thin, this could be a poor, hopelessly dilute Viognier; if rich and with 'legs', this could have enough concentration.

AROMA Assess Viognier above all for intensity of aroma. Wines made from this grape are supposed to burst with peach and apricot, and a boring Viognier just won't do! As well as that ripe, late-summer aroma of peach, expect floral notes too – perhaps honeysuckle.

FLAVOUR Again, lots of that distinctive peach and apricot is needed. There's no excuse for a non-descript, dilute Viognier. A certain rich, mouthfilling texture is important too, as this should not be a watery wine. The acidity should be in good check – enough to give it a fresh zingy lift, but not so much that it tastes tart. Flabbiness is more likely to be a problem, so make sure the acidity is crisp.

FINISH When I drink Viognier, I want that peach/apricot flavour to stay with me long after the wine has gone down. The wine should be rich enough to stand up to fairly rich food too – the likes of creamy chicken curries and pork with fruit sauce. There's a chance your Viognier is oaked – are there any telltale signs of vanilla and spice here? Viognier often divides the critics – some like its distinctive character; others find it too much. Into which camp do you fall?

What did you think?

This tasting offers a good chance to assess whether you prefer rich whites or lighter ones. From the Pinot Grigio and the younger Semillons, which are lighter, crisper wines, to the rich, opulent depths of good quality Viognier and Alsace Tokay-Pinot Gris, the texture and intensity of each white varies considerably. Perhaps you'd simply prefer one of these wines at a summer party, and quite another with a rich, hot meal of spicy chicken. Chances are you had four unoaked whites here - how did they compare to the oaky wines you tried in Stage One? Do you like oaked or unoaked whites, or do they each have their place?

Italy and Spain the heroes

The wines may be called Chianti and Rioja, but the main grape varieties used are Sangiovese and Tempranillo. These are the most famous red wines made in, respectively, central Italy and north Spain. Study the main characteristics of each and, for both pairs of wines, compare the cheaper bottle with the pricier one.

You are tasting...

Inexpensive, light Chianti
Choose cheap Chianti, or any cheap Tuscan red – it may not contain 100% Sangiovese, but the idea is to look at the contrast with the premium Tuscan wine which follows.

More serious, oaky Chianti Classico
Go for something that costs significantly more, and try to pick a Chianti that says 'Classico' on the label, as this means a wine from the better-quality, central part of the region.

Young red Rioja
Buy a red Rioja with *joven* on the label, which means young, or *sin crianza*, which means without barrel ageing. If you can't find one, buy a *crianza* style, which means limited barrel ageing. This wine should be youthful and fairly inexpensive.

Richly oaked, mature red Rioja
Choose a wine that says *reserva* or *gran reserva* on the label – this indicates a wine that has been aged in oak for a long time. It will be older than the previous wine, and it will cost more.

Serve all these wines at room temperature. You don't need to decant them.

1 Inexpensive, light Chianti

APPEARANCE This wine should be a bright, vibrant cherry-red colour, a sign of youth. If it is old and faded, it will have started to turn more brick-brown. Take a good look, and note the texture of the liquid too.

AROMA Tuscan reds, both cheap and expensive, should have a lively aroma of red berries, like strawberries, cherries and plums, jumping out of the glass. There may be a note of tealeaf or tobacco, or even green herbs. But poor examples will merely smell jammy and simple, or even stalky and under-ripe.

FLAVOUR Lots of enticing red berry is needed here, and a good twist of sour acidity. Not too tart, but just enough to give the wine a refreshing, tangy lift. Look out for any other nuances here, but don't expect a lot, as this should be an unpretentious 'quaffing' red – likeable, fruity and medium-bodied.

FINISH Does this wine strike you as easy-drinking and enjoyable? Or is it one-dimensional and boring? In short, is it a crowd-pleaser, or cheap, nasty plonk? A good way to decide is to ask yourself, quite simply, if you'd be happy to drink a couple of glasses. Ask yourself if you'd match it with food, say, red meat or pasta, or if this is a wine to enjoy on its own. Finally, think about the acidity levels – too high, or just right?

2 More serious, oaky Chianti Classico

APPEARANCE This wine is likely to be more richly coloured than the previous one. Hold both glasses up to the light and compare them. Good quality Chianti should have a deep, bright garnet-red hue.

AROMA If this wine is showing off the Sangiovese grape at its best, it will have a lovely summery red-fruit aroma, and lots of other subtle hints too. Expect fresh tealeaves and tobacco, some herbs and sour cherries, almonds, toasted nuts and spicy oak.

FLAVOUR Some Chiantis are much lighter than others, so decide how concentrated and full-bodied your example is, or not. Look out for any signs of oak ageing (cloves, cinnamon, vanilla), as well as that fruity, berryish flavour and the tanginess that goes with high acidity. Does this wine have a lot more flavour than the previous one? Compare it in every sense with the previous wine and consider whether you would pay more money for the flavours you are finding here.

FINISH Check out the acidity on the finish – a nice refreshing lift and a hint of sour cherrydrops are typical of quality Chiantis. How oaky and full-bodied does this wine seem? Will it keep long, do you think, or should it be opened and enjoyed now? Is this an intrinsically 'better' wine than the previous one, or merely different in style?

3 Young red Rioja

APPEARANCE How vivid a red is this wine, as opposed to brown-brick coloured? Is it lively and vibrant in colour, or does it look more mature and mellow than that? It would be interesting to contrast the colour of this wine with that of wine four.

AROMA Which fruit scents are coming through? Perhaps you find red berries again – if so, how do they differ from the aromas of the Italian wines? Perhaps the wine has a more blackcurrant and blackberry perfume. Can you tell that this wine is young – how do you think it might taste different from a mature, older wine?

FLAVOUR How fresh and fruity is this wine? If you have a *joven* or *sin crianza* Rioja, there should be lots of bright berries evident and no oak influence, but if you have a *crianza*, you might find a hint of vanilla or wood spice.

FINISH Think again about oak on the finish, and compare both fruit flavours and acidity with the Italian reds. How mellow is this wine – did you notice a softness or are there some rich, chewy tannins here? How does this wine contrast with the Italian reds you've just tried? Consider if one strikes you immediately as a favourite in terms of flavour and aroma, and maybe go back to the previous two wines to compare them more closely.

4 Richly oaked, mature red Rioja

APPEARANCE This red wine has spent years ageing in oak barrels – can you see any signs of this from its colour? Maturity might have faded the colour from bright red to a more brick or tawny hue – can you spot this here? How rich and dense is the colour?

AROMA Look for signs of long barrel ageing again – is there an oakiness here? Perhaps it shows itself as a vanilla and cream character, or a spicy/pepperiness, or is there an overt sawdust and wood oil smell? Does the aroma have a fresh and fruity quality, or are there more muted, subtle complexities on the nose?

FLAVOUR Note the smoothness of this wine – if it is typical of aged red Rioja it will be soft and mellow. But does that mean the same as 'light'? Decide how intense and full-bodied this wine is. Can you spot strawberries on the palate, or are other fruits present? Can you taste the oak? How does this wine's flavour contrast with that of the previous red?

FINISH It's interesting to note how much a mature, oak-aged wine lingers on the palate, or not. Decide how much oak comes through on the finish, and compare the acidity levels with those of the Italian reds. Is this wine discernibly different from number three? Try to remember what a more mature red tastes like.

What did you think?

Four reds from two countries - two much more simple and inexpensive than the others. On the evidence of this tasting, would you splash out on the more 'serious' reds of Tuscany and Rioja, or would you be happy to stick with the cheaper wines? Decide which occasion each wine would suit - parties, Sunday lunch or fine dining? It is interesting to note the different fruit and oak flavours of each, and to look at the extra maturity of the last wine in contrast with the others.

Semillon master of disguise

Here we take one grape variety and look at the widely contrasting styles of wine it can create. Not just on its own either – some of these wines show Semillon as it is often seen, paired with Sauvignon Blanc. The tasting runs the gamut from bone-dry whites to luscious, sweet ones, and takes in wines from both northern and southern hemispheres.

You are tasting...

Inexpensive, light French Semillon
Find a white from southwest France – Bordeaux, Bergerac, Entre-Deux-Mers – which is 100% Semillon or a blend of Semillon and Sauvignon Blanc (the Semillon should be at least 50%). Choose an inexpensive, very young wine.

More serious, oaky, white Bordeaux
Probably a blend of Sauvignon Blanc and Semillon. Pick a wine with one or two years' maturity, and find one that is oaked – it might say 'barrique' or simply 'oak'. A wine from the Graves area would be ideal.

Pure Australian Semillon
100% varietal wine, preferably from the Clare or Barossa Valleys in South Australia, or from the Hunter Valley in New South Wales. A Semillon from South or North America could be substituted here.

A sweet Semillon – from Bordeaux or Australia
This may come in half-bottles and say 'botrytis' on the label (see page 102). It should be relatively young and orangey-yellow in colour.

Taste all the wines freshly opened and lightly chilled.

1 Inexpensive, light French Semillon

APPEARANCE Don't expect a lot of bright colour here. This wine will almost certainly be pale, but try to spot whether the faint hints of colour are green, yellowy or straw. It may well be thin too. Swirl to find out.

AROMA As with all light, dry whites, this wine should have a very fresh, clean, mouthwatering scent. (That's not the same as a strong perfume, though – this wine will not be pungent.) Expect some freshly cut grass – both Sauvignon and young Semillon have this characteristic – and citrus fruit, probably lemon. Is this aroma boring or enticing?

FLAVOUR Young Semillons or Semillon blends from southwest France tend to have a tangy character with citrus fruit, mainly that of lemon, grapefruit and tangerine. Perhaps there is also a light touch of peach, or even a grassy, almost white pepper hint. It should always taste whistle-clean, with a mouthwatering acidity – be sure to mark it down if that crisp tang is not there. Note the lack of oak too, and keep it in mind when you are tasting the next two wines.

FINISH That crisp, refreshing succulence should win out on the finish of this wine, leaving you with a clean taste in your mouth and, let's hope, wanting more! But don't expect much else. This is a fairly simple white. So as long as it tastes appealingly fresh and fruity with a dry finish, that's fine.

2 More serious, oaky, white Bordeaux

APPEARANCE Compare the colour of this wine with the previous one. Don't forget, this was made from the same grape varieties and in the same region of the same country, France. Yet it should look richer, more buttercup-yellow in hue. It might be a little thicker in texture too.

AROMA Just as the colour is more interesting with this wine, so the perfume should be more deep and complex. If the wine has been fermented and/or aged in new oak barrels, it will have hints of toast, vanilla or even sawdust on the nose. Whether it has or not, the wine should have a fresh lemon aroma that is nicely balanced, and be richer and riper than your first sample.

FLAVOUR This wine has almost certainly cost you more than the previous one, so you want to taste more exciting flavours! The texture should be richer and riper and Semillon's lemon and honey should be there, together perhaps with a little grassiness if the wine is still young. This should be a harmonious wine, well-balanced in its fruit, oak and acidity – in short, a class act.

FINISH Is your wine balanced on the finish, or does one element (fruit, oak, acid) stand out? Do you think it has the potential to age further? Think about the acidity level in particular on the finish, and whether it seems high enough to last the distance. Is the finish totally dry or is there a faint hint of sweetness?

3 Australian Semillon

APPEARANCE This wine will almost certainly be a lot richer and yellowy in colour than wine one, and it may well outshine wine two in its hue. Hold the samples up beside each other to compare the colours, and assess the weight and body of the liquid too.

AROMA After any subtleties experienced with the previous wines, this should have quite a strong and distinctive perfume. Semillon smells of citrus, peach and tinned pineapple, and lime often sings out strongly in Australian examples. Those fruits might seem more ripe and rich than in either of the previous wines, perhaps as a result of warm vineyard viticulture. Look out for signs of oak ageing too – warm, spicy, toasty character – and compare them with any oak characteristics spotted in wine two.

FLAVOUR Ditto the flavour – it should be more vibrant and 'upfront' than the other wines here. A younger example of warm-climate Semillon will be a little grassy, but try to spot that ripe fruitiness again and decide which fruits are here. What about any other nuances – toast, cream, marmalade, beeswax and honey?

FINISH Two questions – is the acidity high enough (Semillon can trail off disappointingly and lack tanginess) and is the finish dry enough? Also assess if this wine is as complex and subtle as wine two. You have probably made some very different tasting notes for this wine – are you starting to build up a picture of Australian styles, and what characteristics are you beginning to associate with this country's wines? Relate your notes to the idea of hotter climates and riper fruit.

4 Sweet Semillon

APPEARANCE Now you can really get going describing the colour of a wine! Sweet Semillon is more concentrated in orangey-yellow hues than the dry versions. Take a close look at the texture of the wine too – it is bound to be richer, thicker and more luscious than any other you have seen so far.

AROMA It should be delectable – full of tropical fruits, dried peel, nuts, marmalade, honey… Let your imagination run wild as you describe the wonderful aroma of this sweet wine. Notice how different the scent is from the dry Semillons.

FLAVOUR With lots of poor, sickly sweet wines on the market, it is essential that this dessert Semillon has plenty of crisp acidity to balance out that sweetness. The wine should be mouth-filling and rich in texture, without being cloying. Note all the intriguing nuances of fine sweet wine – perhaps you find barley sugar, apricots, toasted nuts on the flavour.

FINISH This wine really should linger on and on. It should make your mouth water with its high levels of acidity and sugar, and it should coat your mouth a little with its rich texture. Does your wine do all this? Try to imagine what sort of dish you would match it with – pudding, yes, but which one? And do you think it might go with cheese and even pâtés too?

What did you think?

Some very, very contrasting wines made from
the same grape, albeit one that has perhaps
been blended, in one or two cases, with
Sauvignon Blanc. This is Semillon in its most
familiar guises. It's not the best-known grape
in the world, but now you can appreciate its
versatility! The light dry white, the rich white
and the sweet white – all can be made with
this grape. Which wine impressed you most?
Take price into account when deciding. Try
to devise a four-course dinner party where
you serve each of these wines in turn with
a suitable dish.

Syrah/Shiraz simple to showy

The fact that this grape has two names – Syrah and Shiraz – is a clue to the fact that it produces many different types of wine. It all depends on where it is made, how it is made and who makes it! Here are four wines all created from this variety that reflect a wide range of styles. From juicy, fresh pink to rich, spicy red, this exercise gives you a fascinating insight into a great grape.

You are tasting...

Syrah or Shiraz Rosé
Pick a pink from the south of France made from Syrah (try a Vin de Pays d'Oc from the Languedoc), or a Shiraz rosé from Australia, South Africa, Chile or the US. Chill lightly.

Simple French Syrah
Choose an inexpensive example. Again, Vin de Pays d'Oc Syrah is the most likely candidate. Make sure your label states the grape variety and that it isn't a blend. Serve at room temperature.

Serious Rhône Syrah
Look out for a more expensive wine from a particular part of France's northern Rhône Valley that relies on Syrah (Côte-Rôtie, Crozes-Hermitage, Cornas, St-Joseph). Open an hour or two before tasting (preferably decanting the wine) and serve at room temperature.

Australian or South African Shiraz
Make sure you try a 100% Shiraz from one of the classic Australian wine regions such as Hunter Valley, Barossa Valley or Margaret River, or from South Africa's Stellenbosch or Paarl regions. Serve at room temperature.

1 Syrah or Shiraz Rosé

APPEARANCE Rosés are not all the same shade of pink – this wine will be either lighter or darker than the rosé you tasted in Stage One. It is most likely to be darker, as Syrah produces notably deep pink wines. Does the colour look a bright, almost purpley-pink, or an orangey-pink, which can indicate age? Always look at texture too, to assess if this will be a thin or rich, or possibly even sweet rosé.

AROMA Rosé offers up red-berry flavours like a summer pudding, so expect raspberries, strawberries and cherries. The scent of a rosé should be really enticing, vibrant and freshly fruity, and with Syrah you may get a slight hint of spice, cream, or even light caramel too.

FLAVOUR Plenty of succulent, tangy, relatively light fruit flavours should come dancing on to your tongue. Is there crisp acidity to provide the succulent, mouthwatering character crucial to good rosé? Or do you have a poor, flabby example in your glass? Consider whether your rosé is totally dry or off-dry, and how rich or light it is. Hint: Syrah grapes usually produce quite rich rosés, which can taste sweetly ripe (not sweet, but sweetly ripe, note!).

FINISH Is it a rich and weighty rosé, or a thin and weedy one? Did the flavours finish on a ripe note or a stalky, green one? How did the fruit linger in the mouth? Cast your mind back (or look up your notes) to the rosé tasted in Stage One and compare the two wines. Finally, remember the Syrah characteristics of this rosé – deep colour, red berries, hints of spice and toffee – and see if you spot them again in the reds of this tasting...

2 Simple French Syrah

APPEARANCE Is the colour a rich, dense and dark garnet, or is this a paler style of wine? Tilt the glass and look at the edge of the liquid – would you describe it as deep garnet-red or mahogany? Or does it have a blueish hint to it, indicating youth? Does the colour chime in with the age of the wine? With age, the bluey-purple tone is lost and wine becomes more brick-red... As always, assess texture by swirling the liquid around.

AROMA What does this straightforward, no-nonsense example of French Syrah smell like? Most modern examples have a rich, ripe blackcurrant scent, though you might find it more strawberry or blackberry-ish. Generally speaking, youthful, simple Syrah tastes more of red berries, while the riper, richer ones have black fruit flavours. Look out for other nuances on the nose – pepper, spice, toffee, cream or herbs...

FLAVOUR You should find a good depth of ripe berries here. Modern examples of southern French Syrah tend to have lots of blackcurrant flavour. Some even liken it to black or red wine gums! Don't forget to look out for good, well-balanced acidity, oak character and tannin structure. Think about the wine's texture in general. Is it rich or light? Is this wine perfect for drinking now, or do you think it will keep well for a year or so?

FINISH Is the wine soft and rounded, or does it seem chewy and over-tannic? (Over-extraction is a useful word when it comes to a heavy, over-chewy wine.) Did the flavours linger? Is this red OK to drink on its own, or does it need food?

3 Serious Rhône red

APPEARANCE How does the colour of this wine compare with the previous one? If it is relatively young, it is likely to be richly coloured, implying that the wine will taste concentrated. The colour might be an almost blackish red, and the texture could be very heavy and thick. Older wines will be a little paler, more orange.

AROMA It's fascinating to 'nose' a fine Rhône red. Note all the scents that have nothing to do with the conventional fresh fruit character of wine. There should be an underlying core of cassis or strawberry, but there's so much more going on. Use your imagination, but here are some hints: black pepper, treacle, tar, coffee, chocolate, thyme and rosemary... Think about whether you can smell oak too. Does this seem more complex than the previous wine?

FLAVOUR Look out for more unusual, perhaps 'wilder' characteristics here. Rhône reds can be quite quirky, so expect the unexpected. I have spotted the savoury hints of meat casseroles, wild thyme, even something slightly horsey in Rhône reds. Consider the fruit flavours too, and look out for pepperiness. Think about the concentration of the flavours – these wines can be powerful and rich. Is there oak here? If so, is it in good balance with the other components?

FINISH Assess any tannins after you have tasted the wine. Would you prefer to give it time to age before opening? It will probably leave a lingering flavour, but is it well-balanced overall? Though strong in character, are the elements in balance with one another, or does one (tannin, acidity) stick out like a sore thumb?

4 Australian/South African Shiraz

APPEARANCE Look at the colour in comparison with wines two and three. Note the concentration and the exact shade, blackish red, blueish red or brick red. Consider the texture too, as you roll the wine around the glass. Does it look as big and rich as the previous wine?

AROMA Australian and Cape reds are famous for their rich, fruity qualities. Does this wine live up to that billing? Is there fresher, 'primary' fruit flavour here, and less of the unusual, 'wild' undertones noted in the Rhône wine? I often find a whole heap of cassis in Aussie Shiraz, for example. Look out for chocolate too. Some claim to find eucalyptus, black pepper and even a slightly leathery scent in Aussie Shiraz. Don't forget to assess the oak as well – full-on vanilla and sawdust notes, or subtler than that?

FLAVOUR Warm-climate Shiraz often delivers a concentrated mouthful of fruit, but with a riper, more rounded texture than Rhône reds. Is this what you find, or is your example more angular and tannic? How are those untamed characteristics you may have spotted in the French wines by comparison here? Is this a smooth, velvety, rich wine, or another growling, tannic monster? Do you prefer wine three to this one?

FINISH How does the oak come out on the finish – well-integrated and balanced, or spiky and out of kilter? Is this a wine to drink when young, or does it need time to mellow out? Try to work out when you would drink it. At a barbecue, or with a hearty winter's stew? Could you imagine knocking it back at a party, or is this too heavy and concentrated a wine for that?

What did you think?

Now you have tasted Syrah/Shiraz in four contrasting guises, which wine did you prefer? As always in wine, the grape changes character from country to country, so direct comparison is a great way to get to grips with it. Do you think it makes a good variety for producing rosé? (Think too about the rosé you tasted in Stage One, which was made from Merlot.) And which of the reds stood out for you? There's no right answer here – just work out what suits you best. Consider richness and concentration, balance and complexity. And think about plain 'drinkability'. Sometimes the wines that are most impressive on 'first sip' are not the ones we want to drink for sheer enjoyment. Finally, decide which wines would suit specific occasions, like Christmas, parties, roast Sunday lunch.

Cape crusade four reds

This time the tasting focuses mainly on the place rather than the grape varieties. I've chosen one winemaking region - the western Cape - to demonstrate a variety of wines made in close proximity to each other. Here are four reds, all from one corner of South Africa - and you can bet they will not all taste the same...

You are tasting...

Cool climate Pinot Noir
Most Pinot Noir made in South Africa is produced in the Walker Bay region, close to Hermanus, on the coast. The coastal breezes help to keep the vineyards cool. Pick a Pinot from this area.

Inexpensive, warm climate Cabernet-Merlot
Find a Cabernet, or a Merlot, or a blend of the two from one of the warmer spots in the Cape. Stellenbosch or Paarl are good regions to look for.

Hot climate Shiraz
Pick a Shiraz (also known as Syrah) from any warm part of the Cape.

Blended, premium red from Stellenbosch
Stellenbosch is South Africa's most famous region for reds and many of its top wines come from here. Choose a blend (probably Cabernet-Merlot, but it's up to you) from Stellenbosch and pick an expensive, serious, full-bodied wine.

Taste all these wines at room temperature. You may wish to open the last one and decant it for an hour or two before tasting to let it open out and soften a little.

1 Cool climate Pinot Noir

APPEARANCE Take a look at the colour of the Pinot in your glass. Is it a blueish-red or a deeper mahogany? Check out the thinness – Pinot does not tend to be particularly rich or 'heavy' in texture.

AROMA Swirl and sniff. Do you find here the fresh strawberry fruit typical of Pinot Noir (remember the discussion of this grape in Stage One)? Does it seem enticing and lively, as Pinot should, or just jammy and simple? How sweet is the smell, and do you notice an oaky character?

FLAVOUR Always concentrate on texture with Pinot Noir. Is your wine silky, soft and seductive? Is the acidity high enough to provide a refreshing streak to the wine, or is it too tart? Again, look for specific fruits, such as red cherry, raspberry, strawberry and plum, with hints of oak and perhaps some chocolate or roasted nuts. Is this an attractive, beguiling wine, as Pinot Noir is reputed to be?

FINISH How is that all-important texture on the finish? – good Pinot should always slip down easily without giving a sensation of heavy tannin. Check out the acidity and try to form an opinion on the ripeness levels. Cool vineyards can create elegance, freshness and balance, but they may lead to under-ripeness too. Assess your wine on this basis.

2 Inexpensive, warm climate Cab-Merlot

APPEARANCE This wine may look quite different from the previous one. Cabernet in particular is highly coloured, as we know, so look out for extra density of deep red. Swirl it to see if the liquid is thicker and richer than the previous wine. (It is only a cheap and cheerful red, so it may not be.)

AROMA Different fruit aromas should assail you here. Note the specific smells – blackcurrant, plum, brambles – and try to see how ripe these fruits are. Already, does this wine seem like the product of a hotter vineyard than the previous one? Richer, riper and more 'baked' somehow? How about the oak?

FLAVOUR Cassis and red plums are more likely to be the flavours here, but apply the same thinking as above – does this seem somehow to be a wine made in a warmer vineyard than wine one? Is the wine richer, more rounded and mouthfilling, with less greenness to it? Does it seem more or less elegant than the first wine?

FINISH Check out the flavours at the end of the palate and see how long they linger. This is another chance to think about ripeness and the effects of warm sun. Any oakiness or high acidity or sweet, ripe flavours will come through on the finish, as will a chance to assess the texture for richness and tannins. List the various ways in which this wine differs from the first one. Think about the dishes this would complement.

3 Hot climate Shiraz

APPEARANCE This wine may well be darker in colour and richer in concentration and texture than the previous two. Why do you think that might be? Think up some new words to describe the colour - not just dark red or brown-red.

AROMA Those wilder, spicier aromas from Shiraz should be present, so sniff out any peppery, herby characteristics. How does this aroma seem, in terms of ripeness and exposure to hot sun? Can you tell it came from a warm area and, if so, how?

FLAVOUR The flavours of this wine will be in contrast to those of the previous reds, partly because it is a different grape variety. But compare it to wine one in particular - is it riper, richer, clearly from a warmer area? Perhaps a hint of sweetness gives it away. What do you think it would have tasted like if it had come from a cooler spot? Look out for oak treatment, how the acidity levels compare with the first two wines, and try to decide whether the tannin levels are high or low.

FINISH The flavours of a warm-climate Shiraz should linger on and on in your mouth, but how do they compare with the previous wines? Think about oak, tannin and ripeness in particular. Do you like this wine more or less overall than the first two, or is it a matter of different wines for different occasions?

4 Blended premium red from Stellenbosch

APPEARANCE If this is a young, premium red, and if it is a blend of Bordeaux grapes, it will probably be a very rich but vivid garnet red colour, veering towards inky purple. Compare it with the other three wines and look especially at its texture to see how weighty and rich it is.

AROMA The aroma might be a little closed on this sample - which means it may not have 'come out' fully yet, as the wine is young and tough. If you have decanted it, however, the richness on the perfume may start to waft out a little more. Think about the fruit flavours, the ripeness implied by the bouquet.

FLAVOUR When you are tasting this wine, look not only at the obvious fruit and oak flavours, but assess how hot the vineyards were where the grapes were sourced. Think too about the ageing potential for the wine. Does it seem concentrated and full of flavour, acidity and tannin that is yet to soften and peak, or is it at its best, do you think? Is this wine more exciting and complex than any of the previous three?

FINISH We know this wine came from grapes grown in a hot climate. Contrast it to the first wine - also a high quality Cape red, but made in a cool spot from Pinot Noir. Having tasted through the samples, is it becoming clearer that heat in vineyards plays its part? How have you noticed the finish of the wines changing when you move from a cool-climate wine to a hot-climate one? Refer especially to sweet ripeness, acidity and tannin levels.

What did you think?

We all develop strong opinions about the sort of wines we prefer, but most true wine fans say they appreciate top-quality bottles from both cool and hot vineyards. They might well say that the cooler-climate wines show subtlety and elegance and a streak of fresh acidity, while the hot-climate reds have more power and guts, richer tannins and sweeter, riper, more rounded flavours. Do you agree with this? Having tasted reds from various different parts of the Western Cape, it should be clear that no country or region has one particular 'type' of wine alone – although a particular place may be better at one style than another. Finally, try to match each of the four wines to these dishes – a rich salmon steak; sausage and mash; roast lamb and steak in pepper sauce.

Fighting fizz sparklers

It sounds like great fun, but tasting fizz is surprisingly difficult. The high acidity and the texture of the bubbles both need assessing, and they seem to get in the way when you are looking for quality and subtle flavours. But here are four sparkling wines that should be sufficiently different from one another to make for interesting comparisons.

You are tasting...

Inexpensive Cava
Spain's traditional sparkler from the Penedès region. Choose a cheap version, non-vintage but newly bought and freshly opened – don't taste a tired old bottle. Make sure it is not pink (*rosado*) and that it says 'brut' (dry) on the label.

Non-vintage Champagne
Champagne is only Champagne when it's from the Champagne region of northeast France. Go for a non-vintage wine (no year on the label), and pick 'brut' again. Avoid very expensive, non-vintage Champagnes, as they are too rich to be typical.

New World sparkling wine
California, Australia or New Zealand are the best large-scale producers of 'new-wave' fizz. Don't pick an expensive bottle, or a real cheapie, but something in between. Vintage or non-vintage, it doesn't matter. Again, pick a 'brut' style.

Sweet sparkling wine
Likely to be the widely available Asti or Moscato d'Asti from northern Italy, although Clairette de Die from France would be good too. Make sure it is a sweet sparkler – avoid one that says 'brut'.

Taste these wines lightly chilled.

1 Inexpensive Cava

APPEARANCE Once the froth of pouring the wine has died down, take a good look at the colour of your Cava. How would you describe it – straw, pale green or yellowish? Chances are Cava will look fairly neutral. Have your first serious look at bubbles too – literally assess the size and ferocity of the mousse. Big bubbles or fine little ones? Persistent streams of fizz, or a little flat?

AROMA Cava can smell neutral and boring, but you might discern a light appley aroma, perhaps a hint of yeastiness, or even the 'warm earth' that some claim is in top-quality examples. The wine doesn't need to have a rich aroma to smell fresh and appealing, however. Make sure your Cava does smell suitably fresh, or mark it down.

FLAVOUR No great shakes here, but the flavour should be crisp and fresh, with good tangy acidity on the finish – palate-cleansing, in short. Look out for that crunchy apple (there may be lemon and pears too) and any other subtle undertones, such as creaminess. Think about the bubbles again – are they fine or coarse, flat or ultra-fizzy?

FINISH Assess the acidity levels – you want the Cava to be succulent and a little mouthwatering, but not tart. How do the bubbles seem on the finish – trailing off disappointingly, or lively and invigorating?

2 Non-vintage Champagne

APPEARANCE Hold the glass up next to the Cava. Is this wine a richer colour, and does it seem more viscous and weighty in texture? How do the streams of bubbles compare?

AROMA Good Champagne, even a relatively inexpensive, non-vintage one, should have a little more complexity than Cava. I would look for creaminess, perhaps a hint of yoghurt, and some pineapple and peach to go along with citrus fruit and even some yeasty, bready, toasty notes on the aroma. Freshness should be paramount, with the wine smelling enticing, young and fruity.

FLAVOUR Ditto the flavour. At the very least the wine should be elegant, clean, fruity and fresh, but in a fine example there is something more – some richer notes that indicate the lees ageing. Try to spot some signs of yeast – breadiness, creaminess, even dough or toast undertones. Watch those acidity levels carefully – some cheaper Champagnes taste raw and too tart, when they should be crisp and refreshing.

FINISH Think about the character of the mousse again, compared with wine one – the size of the bubbles and their frequency. How much does this wine linger on the tastebuds compared to the Cava? Finally, can you tell it is made from different grape varieties? Which flavours are dominant? How fresh is the finish? Does it seem tart and sour, or is there just enough refreshing acidity?

3 New World sparkling wine

APPEARANCE How does the colour of this wine compare with the first two? Look out for signs of extra ripeness while tasting this wine, perhaps a slightly richer yellow colour. Check out the bubbles, too – they may not be as fine as those in the Champagne.

AROMA Still wines from the newer wine areas are famous for their ultra-fruity, upfront liveliness, so check out this wine for a similar character. Does it have a fruitier, richer aroma than the European sparklers? Is there any creaminess and yeastiness here, or is it all fruit, fruit, fruit?

FLAVOUR As well as examining those fruity flavours, think about the texture too. Are the bubbles bigger and coarser than the European wines, and how is the acidity level of this wine by comparison?

FINISH Check out those bubbles once more, as they may seem quite different in size and persistency. Do the fruit flavours linger long, and is there an overall sense of ripeness, as though the grapes came from hotter vineyards? Think about the three dry sparklers you have now tasted. Did one stand out as 'better' than the others, or was one especially to your taste? Or can you imagine enjoying two or more of them on particular occasions?

4 Sweet sparkling wine

APPEARANCE After looking at the colour, it's important to check the clarity of the wine and the size of the bubbles. Some sweet fizzes are slightly cloudy, and some have a froth rather than overt fizz, with lots of tiny bubbles.

AROMA Your wine is likely to have been made with the Muscat (or Moscato) grape and should taste quite different to the dry sparklers. Expect some fresh grapes and kiwi fruit aromas, perhaps pears and a dab of honey. Does it smell fresh and natural, or is there an artificial note?

FLAVOUR Again, look out for different fruits, such as green grapes. Is the sweetness in balance with the acidity? There should be plenty of both to give the wine a crisp tang as well as a luscious sugary quality.

FINISH It's really important that a sweet fizz has an appealing mix of crispness and sweetness on the finish, so check that these qualities balance each other in a pleasing way. How do the bubbles feel on the palate – like lots of fine beads, or big and bouncy? Is there a clean, pleasant, tangy end to the wine, or does it leave a fake sickliness in the mouth? Would you prefer to stick to dry sparklers, or is there now also a place in your wine cellar for the odd sweet bottle of bubbly?

What did you think?

Consider the various price points of these wines. Which one do you think represents the best value for money? Is it worth spending more for Champagne, or were you happy with the quality of the cheap Cava or the medium-priced New World fizz? Perhaps the contrasts between these wines surprised you. Do you think one might be more suitable for aperitifs, one to go with seafood, one for everyday parties, and so on? Which desserts do you think would best suit the sweet sparkler?

Buyer's guide

More tips about buying wine, and here we address three topics that can cause some serious angst: ordering wine in restaurants; buying wines from smaller, obscure producers; and buying wine at the cellar door. Overcome your worries and attempt all three with confidence!

Good advice: Restaurants

Many people are nervous about ordering fine wine in smart restaurants. They worry that they will waste their money or embarrass themselves in front of the waiter.

But, if you are dining out for a special occasion and spending a lot of money on great food, it makes sense to browse the upper echelons of the wine list for a fantastic bottle of wine. If you feel intimidated by this, the answer is simple – use your sommelier (wine waiter). Ask for a recommendation with a particular dish, make sure you get a taste before you commit, and always send back a wine that you think is faulty. The wine waiter is a resource, so pick his or her brains before parting with your money.

Remember, it is rarely a good idea to order the house wine. 'House' wine is supposed to be the restaurant's recommended bottle – an appealing, everyday wine that all can enjoy. In truth, it is often mediocre plonk, being fobbed off on customers too nervous to look elsewhere on the list. Often the list only states 'house red – carafe' or 'French vin de pays rouge', which tells you very little. Of course, there are exceptions to this, but unless you know and love the house wine, try to use the main wine list and pick something better and much more interesting.

Beware high 'mark-ups' on restaurant wines – a huge problem. Vote with your feet and shun rip-off restaurants with over-priced wines, or look for BYOs (Bring Your Own) with heart-warmingly low corkage charges... Other signs that a restaurant cares about the wines it serves are a good choice by the glass and cross-references to dishes.

Labels: Smaller producers

On the whole, wines from smaller wineries can be more interesting – individual and 'hand-crafted'. So give them a chance, but be aware that you are taking a small risk. With big names, you tend to get more reliable quality – an obscure label might be obscure for a reason. However, some cheap, big brands can be bland, and fewer single-vineyard wines that reflect *terroir* are produced by huge corporations. It would be sad if the world of wine were taken over by multi-national producers. Find a smaller winery whose bottles you like, and you'll be glad you branched out.

Most of us look for finer wine once we start to delve into this fascinating world, and there are plenty of rip-offs out there, so think carefully before parting with hard-earned money. Let's assume we are talking about wine that is above-average in terms of price, but not sky-high, cult labels. One useful tip is to look for good-value bottles from areas that are not currently fashionable.

Portugal's red table wines are a case in point. Except for its wonderful port, Portugal's reds are under-rated. Try more costly bottles (even these won't set you back much) from the Alentejo, Ribatejo, Dão, Bairrada and Douro regions for some wonderfully concentrated, often surprisingly smooth flavours. Greek wine is also largely ignored, but it is looking highly promising of late. Try the salty-fresh, aromatic whites and the ripe and chunky reds.

Shop alternatives: Buying abroad

If you are visiting a winemaking region anywhere in the world, it is a great idea to visit the 'cellar door' and do some tasting. If you come across a magnificent wine that is not available at home, it clearly makes sense to buy some then and there. However, make sure you'll receive exactly the same wine at home – same blend, same vintage – because a slightly different *cuvée* (bottling) may taste quite different. Whether you stick it in the boot of your car or have it shipped home, make sure that the conditions are suitable, or your wine may be broken or ruined.

Wines in a restaurant cellar: It's usually worth trading up from the house wine, but beware some restaurants' exceptionally high mark-ups.

Drinker's guide

You've mastered the basics about food matching, storing and serving, so here are some more advanced tips about all three subjects. This is the essential lowdown on dinner party wines, storing your bottles before drinking, and the fine art of decanting!

Food matching: Dinner parties

You've learnt quite a bit about matching wine with simple food, but what about posh dinners? How can you show off your best dishes and top wines by marrying them brilliantly? Dinner parties can involve some pretty serious culinary flair, so it stands to reason that your wine choice will crank up a notch, and that you will want your bottles to be exact matches for specific dishes.

Most importantly, think about all the ingredients of each dish, not just the main part of it. For example, if you are cooking chicken in a creamy, lemon sauce, the perfect match is a chilled white Chablis. However, if you stew the chicken in a rich red wine, onion and bacon casserole, then a red such as Chilean Merlot is a much better bet.

Also think about the overall richness and 'weight' of the dish and find a wine to match it. A light grilled Dover sole requires a delicate wine, perhaps a Mosel Riesling, while salmon en croute with a rich butter sauce is better matched to a powerful, oaked New World Chardonnay.

It's a good idea to start a dinner party with a tangy, succulent wine of quite high acidity, to get the tastebuds working. That's why sparkling wines and dry fino or manzanilla sherries work well as aperitifs. Some other sophisticated opening wines are good-quality German Riesling, Sancerre or Pouilly-Fumé (Loire Valley Sauvignon Blancs) or a New Zealand Sauvignon. You can carry this wine through the first course (especially with a vegetarian, fish or seafood recipe), or open a richer white when you sit down to eat.

Most dinner parties will see a richer red being opened with the main course (and even if it's fish, keep a light, slightly cold red available for those who don't want white). Chianti Classico, Rioja Reserva, Australian Cabernet-Shiraz blends, and Merlot from the New World, are all reliably good quality, versatile, food-friendly reds that match a wide range of dishes. If you are serving a big, hearty main dish such as roast red meat, steak or a very rich casserole, you'll need to roll out a bigger gun in the form of a powerful red like Châteauneuf-du-Pape, New World Shiraz or Barolo.

Don't forget the dessert and cheese stages - it is really impressive to serve glasses of sticky pudding wine, port or sweet Malmsey Madeira. You don't need a lot, as these wines are ultra-concentrated in flavour and most guests will just want a taste. Half a bottle should suit four sensible people.

Storage: Unopened bottles

It's not easy to work out how long your unopened wine will stay fresh, and many tired, fruitless and oxidised wines are the result. The fact is, certain styles of wine do need drinking up soon after purchase. To complicate matters, some wines improve with age, needing time in bottle to soften and mellow. Sometimes the information on the back label gives advice on this, but often there's nothing clear to indicate the length of time an unopened bottle will last.

Some tips: to enjoy them at their best, open light, dry and off-dry whites, rosés and inexpensive sparkling wines soon after purchase, or within a couple of months. The same for dry pale fino and manzanilla sherries, the lightest, softest reds like Beaujolais and cheap, insubstantial reds like bargain *vins de table* (France) or *vinos de mesa* (Spain).

Surprisingly, the same can be said for some powerful wines, which are deliberately aged at the winery and released ready to drink. Rioja Reservas and Gran Reservas (the mature versions) are such cases, as the wine matures in barrel and bottle before being sold and should taste mellow enough as is. Tawny port is another example - it is only bottled and sold after spending years languishing in oak casks. Be careful not to keep these wines too long.

Medium-bodied reds, powerful whites such as rich Chardonnays, cheaper dessert wines and top non-vintage Champagnes can be kept for several months or a year before opening. Wines that may benefit from keeping for several years include quality claret, red burgundy, vintage Champagnes and sparklers, vintage port, tannic Rhône and New World reds and sweet wines of France and Germany.

Serving: Decanting

What should you do with a bottle of rich red wine or port that has thrown a sediment? Should you throw the wine away? Absolutely not! This is often the sign of a great, powerful wine that hasn't been filtered, and has dropped a deposit of tannin and other material at the bottom of the bottle while the liquid softened and mellowed. You may have a delicious wine, the problem is how to get it out and leave the sediment. You need a clean glass decanter.

Make sure the bottle has been standing (or lying) still, so that the sediment has collected in one place. Pour the wine slowly, cautiously, into the decanter, preferably in front of a bright light so you can see when the sediment starts to move forward. When it's close to pouring out, stop decanting and throw the dregs away.

stage 3

We've covered many of the basics of wine in stages one and two, so here's where things get more serious. Use the tasting skills and foundation of knowledge you've gained from earlier parts of the book to try some rare and fine wines, fortified and sweet wines. Here we will look more closely at the effect of different vineyard sites on the wine in your glass, and more on buying, serving and storing wine should put you firmly in the picture.

A delicious dozen

It's impossible to cover all the many grape varieties in this book, but here I've picked a further twelve which are important to get to know. They didn't make it into the earlier sections of the book for various reasons – either they are not planted as widely as the varieties you have already encountered, or perhaps they make wine of too variable quality to be counted in the 'premier' league. Or they create unusual, offbeat styles of wine, such as sherry and port.

But don't dismiss the grapes that follow. They each make a valuable contribution to the wonderful variety in the world of wine and I strongly recommend you try each and every one. It would be sad indeed if we all stuck to one or two grapes when we chose our wine, never exposing ourselves to the extraordinary range of flavours out there. And now, of course, you are familiar with the twelve varieties introduced in Stages One and Two, so it is fascinating to compare and contrast this new tasting material! Keep building up your framework of reference, as this is the only way to become familiar with wine and discover your very own likes and dislikes.

Tasting doesn't end here, either. There are other grapes out there that are worthy of exploration. Don't let the end of this book stop you – by the time you have completed the tasting exercises in Stage Three, I hope you will be keen to go out and try some more obscure varieties and blends of grapes. Never stop tasting new grape vines and combinations of vines, or indeed, wines from new regions and producers.

Chenin Blanc

I've waited until Stage Three to introduce Chenin Blanc, partly because it fits in well with the dessert wine explanation that follows shortly (page 102), and partly because although this white grape can make impressive, rapier-sharp dry wines and gorgeously luscious sweet ones, it also produces a lot of dross. It doesn't always live up to the premier league, in my view. Maybe you will find it more consistently enjoyable!

Chenin Blanc enjoys its finest moments in the Loire Valley, where it makes a wide range of styles from the bone-dry, whistle-clean Savennières (which is best cellared for up to twenty years), to the refreshing, sherbetty sparkling Saumur, and the dazzling dessert wines Côteaux du Layon, Bonnezeaux and Quarts de Chaume. It also makes Vouvray both great and grotty (pick and choose carefully from good vintages) and humble, basic Anjou Blanc. Expect a floral aroma, and character of fresh green apples, walnuts, honey and citrus in good examples; wet wool and mustiness in poor ones.

Chenin also makes palatable and appealing, if simple, dryish white wines in South Africa that taste more immediately fruity (think lime and guava). A few excellent examples made from low-yielding vines have appeared recently and standards generally seem to be on the up in the Cape.

Gewurztraminer

If you have never encountered Gewurztraminer before, boy, are you in for a surprise! It has a highly distinctive perfume with wafts of rosewater, lychee, ginger, peach and Turkish Delight. Some describe its heady fragrance as spicy (indeed, the prefix 'Gewurz' means spice). Its wines are never oaked, instead they major on fresh peach, apricot and citrus fruit, sometimes fat, full and rich, at other moments more refreshing and mineral in tone. It's great at blind tastings, as you are unlikely to miss it!

In the Alsace region of eastern France, this golden and pink-skinned grape is a major player, with wines often made in the richly coloured, riper, sometimes sweet, more oily style. There are some truly great bottles, but watch out for ones with low levels of acidity, which can taste flabby and unbalanced. Outside Alsace, Germany makes a more lean and fresh style of Gewurztraminer, northern Italy makes lighter, fragrant whites from it and the occasional cheap gem pops up from Hungary. It does well in cooler areas of newer wine regions, especially vineyards in Chile and New Zealand's South Island. Do try chilled Gewurztraminer with light, spicy Thai dishes – it goes especially well with fish, coriander, lime and lemongrass.

Macabeo/Viura

You may not have heard of this grape under either of its names, but you have almost certainly drunk wine made from it. Macabeo is grown widely across the French/Spanish border, from the Languedoc to Penedès on the Spanish East Coast, and as Viura it is the main white grape of the Rioja region in the Northeast of Spain. It doesn't create wine with any great character, but the best white Riojas made from it have an appealing floral note, and crystal-clear fruity quality, mainly peach. It is one of the three main grape varieties used to make Cava, which is produced in Penedès.

Muscat

It's amusing that so few grape varieties produce wine that is described as 'grapey'. Muscat is the exception – a fresh, dry, young Muscat definitely smells and tastes of crunchy green grapes. Dry Muscat is well worth trying, and the best examples come from the white wine wizards of Alsace. Here they often partner it with fresh asparagus or quaff it cold as an aperitif. Some riper, kiwi-flavoured dry Muscats pop up from the New World too.

But the generic name Muscat covers a whole family of grape varieties, and its scions are responsible for myriad styles of wine. The frothy and frivolous Asti and Moscato d'Asti of Northern Italy are made from Muscat, as are the sweet fortified *vins doux naturels* of southern France such as Muscat de Beaumes-de-Venise. And try the much darker, more toffeed liqueur Muscats of Australia. These are all made from Muscat á Petits Grains. Its close relation, Muscat of Alexandria, creates sweet wines in Spain and Portugal, including the popular Moscatel de Valencia, and is also known as Hanepoot in South Africa and Zibibbo in Sicily. Now you know!

Palomino Fino

Try a glass of Palomino and all you will find is a rather bland white wine with little discernible character. But in one part of the world this variety truly shines – Palomino is the variety behind almost all sherry production. It grows in the white chalky soils around the town of Jerez in Andalucia, southern Spain, and once made into the basic white wine and fortified, is stored in barrels, where a creamy blanket of natural yeast known as *flor* forms on its surface. This gives the wine a characteristic and unique tanginess, saltiness, breadiness...

The result is fino or manzanilla, pale dry sherries or, if the wine is allowed to oxidise, amber coloured, nutty amontillado - great classic wines, without doubt. Avoid Palomino from any other source, however, because it really can't do anything interesting without the natural benefits of the Jerez area. For further explanation of the sherry process, see page 107 in this section of this book.

Pinot Blanc

This is a grape that offends very few people and, while it may never set the world alight, it can be credited with making a great deal of pleasant, easy-drinking, food-friendly white. The best bottles of Pinot Blanc come from Alsace, where a certain apple and melon freshness and slight creaminess shine through. In Germany, it is called Weissburgunder and is sometimes oak-aged for extra body and character.

As Pinot Bianco, it makes refreshing whites in northern Italy, and the Austrians can coax some racy, lean character out of it. Sometimes the fairly neutral, but snappy Pinot Blanc/Bianco is used for sparkling wine, and these are on the whole, quite pleasant, crisp bottles of fizz. The Californians have made one or two oaky, but sprightly *cuvées* with Pinot Blanc. The top Alsace examples are notably easy to match with food - try Alsatian Pinot Blanc with onion tart, ham quiche or braised fennel, for example.

Cabernet Franc

Poor old Cabernet Franc suffers from being confused with Cabernet Sauvignon - or for those who do know the difference, it falls down because it does not produce such great wines. Indeed, Cabernet Franc is often described as the third red grape of Bordeaux, after Cabernet Sauvignon and Merlot, and so it is usually used as a lesser component in the blend. Why use it at all? Well, it does bring a certain fragrance to the claret blend - a fresh fruity aroma with earthy, woodland hints.

But, in the cooler Loire Valley further north, it can make superb red wines all on its own. Soft, refreshing reds with a lovely summery aroma of fresh raspberries, currant-bush leaves and hints of green raw capsicum. These could be just the thing if you are fed up with all-powerful, hefty, tannic wines. A few Cabernet Francs are made successfully in South Africa, California and New Zealand. A grape that is well worth a try in blends and on its own.

Grenache

I like Grenache. It may not have the sophistication or complexity of Cabernet Sauvignon, Pinot Noir or Syrah, but there is something in the rugged honesty and sheer quaffability of its reds that makes it appealing. It used to be thought of as the workhorse red variety of Spain and southern France, churning out oceans of rough plonk - the grape behind so much cheap holiday red and rosé. The Aussies used and abused it too, making some of their roughest reds from it.

But today Grenache is appreciated more by canny winemakers, who buy in low-yielding crops and try to give it a bit more attention in the winery, making the most of its juicy red berry, cherryish fruit flavours and trying to get a twist of spice and pepper in the wine. Now there is plenty of decent Grenache around in Southern France, and it is still a mainstay of the blend in the Southern Rhône, where the wines have impressed more and more of late. The story is the same in Spain, where, as Garnacha, it generally makes better quality red these days, and also some delicious *rosado*. Meanwhile, certain new wave Australian and Californian winemakers are cutting a dash with blends of Grenache, Syrah and Mourvèdre, and occasionally single varietal wines too.

Malbec

This is one of the lesser grape varieties of Bordeaux, where it is known as Cot. Totally obscure, I know, and only some of you will have come across Malbec from the area around Cahors, further east, where it makes dark, powerful, richly tannic red wines. Do try them if you come across them, but not on their own - get a hearty roast on the go first.

Most of us will know Malbec as Argentina's recent success story, and as the grape that has put the area around the city of Mendoza firmly on the international vinous map. Argentina has more plantings of Malbec than anywhere else, and makes its very own style of red from it – concentrated but not heavily tannic, rather velvet-smooth, with a seductive flavour of ripe black cherry. Some bottles of Argentine Malbec are fairly simple and fruity, others have a more chunky, oaky character. But there's no doubt that this has become a modern-day classic. It is rarely seen elsewhere, although the Australians and the New Zealanders use it successfully for its dark colour and natural richness as a blending partner with other red grapes.

Nebbiolo

We have already come across Sangiovese, the great Italian grape of Tuscany. Nebbiolo is the equivalent further north, in Piedmont, and is responsible for making the majestic Barolos and Barbarescos of this hilly, fog-bound region around Alba. The grape makes wines which are tough and tannic when young, but which soften up gracefully over long periods to make fascinating bottles which have a lovely perfume (some say of roses), and complex flavours of black fruit, truffles, liquorice, spicy wood. These wines are truly impressive, but be warned, they do come with high price tags attached.

Nebbiolo is also planted in Lombardy and further south near Brescia. Little is seen outside Italy, although some enterprising Californians (who call themselves the Cal-Itals!) and Australians are giving Nebbiolo a go, as are a few Argentinians.

Touriga Nacional

The vineyards of the Upper Douro Valley in Northern Portugal hold several different varieties for making the port blend, but the best of these is widely considered to be the somewhat formidable Touriga Nacional. This vine produces small crops of little, thick-skinned grapes and wine which has an intense red-berry flavour (plum, cherry) and loads of tannin. The structure and concentration have been compared with Cabernet Sauvignon. These qualities, of course, are ideal for helping to create the rich complexities of port. (See page 107 for more on port production.) You simply couldn't use a weedy, dilute red for this task!

As well as making the most important contribution of any grape to the complex port blend, Touriga Nacional is used for (unfortified) table reds in the Dão region of Portugal, and it occasionally pops up in other countries, namely Australia, for local fortified wines.

Zinfandel/Primitivo

Californian 'Zin' is increasingly popular, but not in the way it used to be. As white or 'blush' Zinfandel, it was invariably used to make weedy pale pink wines with a faint sugariness, and was easily dismissed by serious wine drinkers. Now it has been rehabilitated as a vine used to make rich, ripe, fruity red wines, concentrated and delicious. Californian red Zin has a generous flavour of blackberry, raspberry and strawberry, with spicy, peppery notes to boot. The top examples, from ancient vineyards in Sonoma County and the Sierra foothills, are intense and fascinating. Cheaper, mass-produced red Zins are generally attractive, with moreish, sweetly ripe fruit and some creamy oak; the perfect reds for posh barbecues.

Zinfandel is rarely seen outside California, although it was recently posited that it is the direct descendent of Primitivo, Southern Italy. Some of the best Primitivos do indeed taste a lot like Zinfandel, but there are still some doubts about test results. One or two impressive Zinfandels are made in Australia and Chile.

The vineyard

By now I hope it has been demonstrated dramatically in the tastings that several factors in the vineyard have a huge bearing on the character of the wine in your glass. Climate, soil, man's influence – no two vineyards are the same and thus the results vary considerably. One particular style of wine is a great example of this: sweet botrytised wine. Botrytis? Read on to discover how an unusual set of natural circumstances can lead to the creation of grapes with a very distinctive character...

Sweet wines – what rot!

Although there are plenty of rots and moulds that grape growers do not want to see in their vineyards, there's one type that some actively encourage. *Botrytis cinerea* is a form of mould that attacks ripe grapes in the autumn, shrivelling them on the vine and turning the fruit into unattractive, rather furry sub-raisins, the sort

Grapes affected by the noble rot (Botrytis cinerea) may look unappealing, but the juice they yield up is especially concentrated, unctuous and sweet.

of thing we would normally chuck out of the fruit bowl. But in doing this, the botrytis mould sucks away much of the water inside the grape, concentrating the liquid that is left, intensifying the sugar and acidity and leaving a syrupy gloop.

The wine that is made from this liquid has a special character. It is sweet and unctuous, full of honey and, to balance that out, fresh acidity. There are layers of apricot, peach, citrus and marmalade, but more exotic, off-beat notes too – barley sugar, beeswax, even hints of the mould in the form of mushrooms, warm earth, dried fruits, figs and quince. The list is endless. Botrytis, otherwise known as 'noble rot', adds its own character to the wine and produces a fascinating mouthful of luscious complexity.

But the right conditions are needed for noble rot to thrive. The best 'rotten' vineyards are near a body of water, and ideally, there will be night-time and early morning mists which burn off during the day. The best grape varieties for the job are those with thin skins and high natural acidity, such as Semillon, Chenin Blanc, Riesling. The places where all this comes together with regularity to produce the finest botrytis dessert wines are Bordeaux's Sauternes and Barsac regions; the vineyards of the Loire river valley; those of Germany's Rhine and Mosel; Austria's Neusiedlersee; and Northeast Hungary, where the wonderful sweet wine Tokaji is made.

Even in these prized vineyards, botrytis doesn't always strike with great regularity or uniformity, so you can see why botrytised dessert wines are in great demand and why they fetch high prices. It is essential to try them as you learn about wine – they are quite unique elixirs, conjuring up fascinating smells and flavours, and they speak very clearly of the particular place, vintage and set of natural circumstances in which they were made. Oh, and because of their high levels of sugar and acidity, they live on for years and years, taking on more and more complexity and mellow, marmalade magnificence with age. Get tasting them on page 114.

Heat and ice

In the absence of noble rot, there are other ways to make sweet wine, and most of them involve harvesting extra-ripe grapes that have been allowed to hang on the vine for longer than usual. This usually happens in hot, arid areas where the appearance of botrytis is unlikely. But, if you pass a vineyard in the late autumn and see bunches of somewhat shrivelled, raisiny grapes still hanging on the vines, you can be pretty sure they are destined to become 'late harvest' sweet wines.

One more permutation is Eiswein or Ice Wine. This involves heading out into the vineyards in the dark small icy hours of winter mornings and plucking the over-ripe fruit berry by berry, when the liquid in the grapes is frozen. By squashing those icy little beads and making wine from the thick, semi-slushy liquid that comes out, you end up with a fantastically clean, pure, fruity essence of sweetness and grapiness. Expect a very high price for Ice Wine – well, wouldn't you charge a lot if you had suffered sleep deprivation and frostbite for your pains?

Vintages

Some vineyards with great potential for producing fine wine suffer badly in poor years, only to bounce back with peak condition fruit when the conditions are right. That's why vintages can be important. Back in Stage One I promised more on vintages, so here it is. To recap briefly – don't worry too much about picking specific vintages if you are buying cheap and cheerful quaffing wine, or wine from areas which don't show much of a swing in conditions from year to year. But now we have reached Stage Three, there's a high chance you are looking at finer and pricier wines from classic regions where vintage variation really does matter. This small section, of a book which is fundamentally a tasting course, can't tell you all there is to know about

Region	Fine vintage									
Bordeaux (red)	2002	2001	2000	1995	1990	1989	1988	1986	1985	1982
Bordeaux (white)	2001	2000	1996	1995	1990	1986				
Bordeaux (sweet)	2001	1998	1997	1996	1995	1990	1989	1988		
Burgundy (red)	2002	2001	1999	1995	1993	1990	1989	1988	1985	1978
Burgundy (white)	2002	2000	1997	1996	1995	1986	1985	1978		
Port	2000	1997	1994	1991	1985	1983	1977	1970	1966	1963
Germany	2001	1999	1998	1996	1995	1993	1990	1989	1988	
Loire	2002	2001	2000	1997	1996	1995	1990	1989	1988	
Rhône (red)	2001	2000	1999	1998	1995	1990	1989	1988	1985	
Rioja	2001	1999	1996	1995	1990	1989	1985			

every year and every region, so consider investing in a vintage pocket book for more detail. However, as some of the tastings that follow look at premium classic wines, here is a brief low-down on the exceptional vintages from the key wine regions:

On the whole, the newer wine-producing regions such as Australia, South Africa and California have vintages which show less variation (some argue the wines are less complex and interesting, too!) and conditions tend to be warm, sunny and dry most years. But there are exceptions. New Zealand has distinctly cool-climate regions, and when the weather is inclement and chilly the wines suffer, although they can be fabulous when the climate is kind. The quality of Marlborough whites made in 2001 and 2003 is excellent; Hawke's Bay reds excelled in 1996, 1998 and 2003. In South America, especially Argentina, the effects of El Niño in 1998 were devastating, and 2002 was a cool, rainy and hopeless year for wine in Chile. Think about vintage variation when you are tasting wine.

Clones

Clonal selection of vines may sound like something out of *The Day of the Triffids*, but read on, as it is responsible for much improvement in vineyards around the world. This is the practice of alighting on one individual plant which has a particular attribute, and taking cuttings from it for propagation.

This way, grape growers can achieve, among other factors, better ripeness levels, more resistance to disease, or the sort of yields they require for their style of wine. Many vineyards in the mid-twentieth century had far too many diseased, atypical vines, but in the modern age, clonally selected vines have meant a rise in quality. South African vineyards are a good example. The red wines of this country have improved dramatically in recent years, largely because better, clonally selected vines have been grown.

Professional tasters can often tell the difference between wines made from particular clones, especially when the grape variety used shows clear variation from clone to clone (like Pinot Noir). But for the amateur wine taster, there is no need to worry about this – the label won't tell you anything about a clone anyway. Just be grateful that clonal selection has made such a difference to the standard of vines in today's global vineyards.

Biodynamic viticulture

One step on from organic viticulture is the practice of what the French call 'biodynamie', a distinctly spiritual (some would say 'new age') concept which looks at the relationship between the vineyard, the balance of its soil, and its relationship with the cosmos. Biodynamic vinegrowers closely follow the position of the moon and stars and plan their farming practices around this natural calendar, believing they must listen to the forces of nature when making decisions to plant, to prune or to harvest.

Although they use a couple of basic pesticides against mildew, they reject other 'cides' and artificial fertilisers, turning instead to natural resources such as dung compost, horn compost and horn silica (which they believe aids photosynthesis). They might also use homeopathic cures for disease. New converts claim to see a vast improvement in their vines, and it is interesting to note that biodynamic grape growing is not the preserve of the obscure and hopelessly eccentric – it is practised at such star estates as Domaine Leroy in Burgundy, Chapoutier in the Rhône and Huet in Vouvray.

Sustainable viticulture

Being an old cynic, I suspect the positive results seen by biodynamic farmers is simply because they are paying far more attention to their land, and giving it an awful lot of tender, loving care. I'm more excited by the widespread adoption of sustainable viticulture, which is less way-out than biodynamic and less rigorous than organic viticulture, but which still aims to avoid much damage to the environment.

Under this realistic system, chemical use is severely reduced and often avoided altogether, although there are no strict rules about using some sprays if necessary. Ecological diversity in the vineyard is encouraged, and natural predators (insects) are introduced to keep pests at bay. Green, natural cover crops are grown between vines to help soil fertility, and ploughing rather than herbicides are used. A forward-thinking vineyard owner who embraces sustainable viticulture is also likely to be keen on recycling, using renewable energy sources and even thinking more carefully about the welfare and safety of vineyard workers.

Sauvignon Blanc vines which have been 'spur' pruned, leaving two canes where the bunches of grapes grow.

In the winery

Fortified wines

Two of the important grape varieties used for fortified wines, Palomino Fino (sherry) and Touriga Nacional (port), were introduced earlier in this stage (see The grapes, page 99). So, how are fortified wines actually made? These unusual wines are the products of a long evolution in winemaking methods, over centuries and many generations.

Fortified wines are so called because they have pure grape spirit added to them. This has more than one advantage. It helps to preserve the wine, which is partly how these styles evolved, as they were exported by ship across wide tracts of the globe and needed to remain fresh. Although delivery is much quicker nowadays, this is still helpful, because fortified wines also remain in good condition for longer than table wines once opened – especially madeira, which is virtually indestructible! Then the spirit helps form the style of the wine – stronger in alcohol, obviously, but often sweeter too, as the yeast that turns sugar into alcohol is destroyed when the spirit is added. The unused sugar remains in the liquid, hence the sweeter style of port.

That said, fortified wines are not as powerful as you might think. Or, rather, table wines are perhaps closer in strength than is commonly supposed. A rich New World Chardonnay or Shiraz, from a warm vineyard where the grapes have reached their full ripeness, will often contain around 14.5% alcohol. A dry fino sherry might typically contain 15.5%. So don't blame your hangover entirely on the small sip of sherry you enjoyed during an evening awash with ultra-strong new wave table wines...

Port comes from the dramatically beautiful Douro Valley in northern Portugal, where for centuries the vines have clung to precipitous, rocky slopes, producing small, thick-skinned berries that make a concentrated and tannic red wine. The vineyards contain a range of local Portuguese varieties, of which Touriga Nacional is considered the most important. Historically, port grapes

The beautiful, steep-sided Douro river valley in Northern Portugal is where port is made. The vineyards hold a variety of red grapes from which the blend for port is produced.

were crushed by foot in huge stone tanks, but today most of the crop is mechanically processed.

After the spirit is added, the wine is developed either into a red style of port, the simplest of which is fiery, cherryish ruby, followed by Late Bottled Vintage (the poor man's vintage port, bottled ready to drink from a lesser year), single quinta port (from just one vineyard), or vintage port, the most serious style, usually the best grapes from a 'declared' fine year and bottled while young. Vintage port is normally made only every three or four years, and it needs time to mature in the bottle before drinking – anything from ten to forty years. At its best, it is an extraordinarily intense mouthful of sweet red berries, fruitcake, spice, chocolate and nuts. Tawny ports are aged in oak barrels for ten, twenty or more years, and are much more mellow and nutty in character. They can be brilliantly smooth and moreish. No fine port is particularly cheap, but LBV, single quinta and ten-year-old tawny arguably represent the best value for money.

Sherry comes from around the city of Jerez in Andalucía, Southern Spain. Many people still associate it with one style alone – the sweet, sticky variety, served at room temperature by Great Aunt Gladys at Christmas. The Spanish would rarely drink this – they usually drink their sherry fresh and often chilled, and more dry and tangy, in the form of the surprisingly light and refreshing fino and manzanilla, the driest styles that have unusual 'wake-me-up' aromas and flavours of bitter lemon, green olives and freshly baked bread...

Sherry is made when a natural yeast called *flor* grows a coating over a rather bland base wine, shielding it from oxygen and giving it a distinctive tangy character. Amontillado, a medium amber sherry, is made when the wine is fortified further, the yeast is killed off and the wine becomes oxidised, acquiring a nutty, fruity quality. Oloroso is an even richer, raisin-like version. Sherry is aged in a *solera* system – in the *bodega* (winery), rows of oak casks are layered one above the other. The finished sherry is drawn off the bottom layer, and these casks are topped up from the barrel above, which is in turn topped up from the barrel above that. This means that the final blend contains a fraction of many other sherries of different ages.

Madeira is the great traditional fortified wine from the Portuguese island of the same name. It is heated slightly during a long ageing process, which gives it a caramel character and preserves it wonderfully.

Wines from dried grapes

There is another type of traditional, but unusual, exotic wine. This time it is made from grapes which have been dried before crushing, which concentrates the juice, making it extra-sweet and high in acidity and leading to a luscious, intense wine. This method is a particular speciality of Italy, where the style is known as *passito*. There are sweet *passito* wines, including the famous Italian dessert wine Vin Santo and the *recioto* styles such as Soave Recioto (a sweet, honeyed version of the well-known dry white Soave), and there are dry styles, such as Amarone. Red Amarone wines can be splendid. Valpolicella's Amarone is very rich indeed, with bitter chocolate and fig flavours, and a powerful dose of alcohol.

A few other countries are now attempting the *passito* style. In Austria, dessert wines are sometimes made from dried grapes, and in France some wine is created from fruit which has baked on straw mats in the sun, a style known as *vin de paille*. I have even tasted a passito-style dessert wine made in South Africa, and it was surprisingly good.

Machinery

Thankfully, we haven't yet got robots to make our wine (though it may only be a matter of time). But there are some fancy pieces of winery equipment that make winemakers' lives a lot easier these days. Take the *gyropalettes*, which are increasingly used to make sparkling wines and champagnes. The 'riddling' process of ageing fizz described in Stage Two, when bottles are gradually turned by hand each day over a matter of many months is incredibly time-consuming and expensive. So, unsurprisingly, a machine has been invented to do the job instead. The large, box-like container takes dozens of bottles of fizz and lifts them high in the air (it looks almost like a fairground ride), turning them by minute fractions each day. The results seem to be just as good as hand-riddling.

Results are not quite as impressive for the new metal 'feet' being employed in Portugal to tread the grapes for port, although they are better than automatic crushers. The silver paddles move up and down great vats of fruit during port vintage time, and mimic the gentle but persistent action of traditional foot treading. Experts believe they are almost as good as feet, and they are less expensive than labourers (and never get bunions).

Then there is the reverse osmosis machine, currently all the rage in Bordeaux. This is seriously complex technology and is used when the year is particularly wet. The machine sucks water out of over-plump grapes, thus avoiding the dilute wines that might have been the result otherwise. Critics say the wines made in this way are not entirely natural and even taste too thick and heavy, but drinkers may relish the chance to avoid the rain like never before!

Labels

The bottling and packaging is often done at the winery, so this is as good a time as any to take a quick look at the standard of wine labels. Some of the information on a bottle is useful. Expect to be told the alcohol level (this ranges widely from wine to wine); the vintage (or lack of one, for non-vintage blends); the country and region of production; the grape variety or blend (this doesn't always appear, or it may be on the back of the bottle). Some labels inform you if the wine has been aged in oak, others give helpful facts about the climate, the vintage, the method of production and the best food matches.

Some even have a clear and accurate tasting note – but most don't. Frankly, a lot of back labels are filled with drivel about the 'condors that soar over the mountain peaks' while the vineyards 'nestle in the foothills'. Not exactly helpful. Use the facts that make sense to you and forget the marketing hype. Whether you are looking at the label while you taste, or after a blind tasting, there are probably a few facts there that are illuminating.

Modern technology means new machinery is taking on some of the winery jobs traditionally done by hand (and foot!). Here, automatic gyropalettes slowly rotate bottles of sparkling wine, replacing the need for hand-turning (see page 64).

Classic France the whites

Here are four classic French whites that not only showcase the grape variety used (each one is 100% single varietal), but also reflect closely the soil and climate of the region where the grapes were grown. These are 'must-taste' wines – no serious wine connoisseur should leave these unsampled.

You are tasting...

Sauvignon Blanc from the Loire
Choose a Sancerre or a Pouilly-Fumé – both are 100% Loire Valley Sauvignon Blanc. Pick a fairly young wine and a good, reputable producer. Aim for the medium to high price bracket if possible.

Chablis
A white burgundy from the northern Chablis region. This will be 100% Chardonnay grapes, and should be fruity and lightly oaked. Again, pick a youngish wine, but not from the bottom of the bargain basement – you are after classic quality.

Dry or off-dry Vouvray
Back to the Loire for the most famous white wine made from the Chenin Blanc grape. Vouvray can be very sweet, so avoid a bottle with *moelleux* on the label – you want dry or medium-dry for good comparison with the others. Avoid the cheapest.

Gewurztraminer from Alsace
Look for Alsace bottles – tall, green and Gothic. The grape Gewurztraminer will appear on the label. Pick a good producer – Zind-Humbrecht, Trimbach, Hugel or Turckheim – and make sure your wine is youthful or it won't compare well.

Taste all these wines after chilling them lightly.

1 Sauvignon Blanc from the Loire

APPEARANCE This wine will be pale, perhaps with a light straw or green hint. But it should look clear, light and fairly thin.

AROMA Swirl, sniff and you can expect a bracingly fresh lemon aroma, perhaps with other more subtle connotations. There might be a mineral hint – hard to define in words, but a little stony, chalky or even a trace of smoke. The 'fumé' of Pouilly-Fumé refers to this trait, often described as being a little like gunflint or pistol smoke. It is supposed to reflect the chalky soils of the region – can you spot it?

FLAVOUR It should be very clean, mouthwatering and dry – also check that the acidity of your wine is in balance. Not too tart, but nice, fresh and zesty. You may well find some citrus flavour, but which fruits exactly, and what about anything else? Do you notice the mineral/chalk/smoky attribute on the flavour?

FINISH How is the acidity and dryness on the finish? Is this wine a long, lingering one, or a short, disappointingly weak one? Try to remember how dry it is when comparing it with the wines that follow. And think back to other dry whites you tasted in Stages One and Two, perhaps referring to tasting notes. How does this one strike you as different, and is it one you would like to drink in the future? How long do you think it would keep, unopened? Do you think this wine could be described as good-value for money?

2 Chablis

APPEARANCE This should make an interesting comparison with the previous wine – the colour may be similar, but it is likely that the Chablis will be a slightly deeper gold.

AROMA As this white is made from Chardonnay, rather than Sauvignon Blanc, it will have a different fruit aroma (which fruits? Citrus? Tropical?) and Chardonnay tends to be richer, riper, more rounded in both smell and flavour. That said, Chablis in northern Burgundy is a relatively cool climate area, so bear in mind that this might be a light and elegant take on the grape...

FLAVOUR ...which you will notice on the flavour too – fruity and rounded, but not too rich, overpowering or mega-oaky. Rate the richness and body. Can you taste apples or oranges? Is there a hint of toasty/buttery oak here? What about any subtle influence from the Kimmeridgian soil of the Chablis region, which is quite chalky and said to give a mineral hint to the wine?

FINISH How does the finish compare with the Sauvignon Blanc, thinking especially about acidity levels, length of flavour and oaky character? Is this a richer, fuller wine overall, and which dishes would it go with? Decide if this wine shows the freshness, fruitiness and sophistication that many associate with Chablis. Or is it just another dry white wine?

3 Dry or off-dry Vouvray

APPEARANCE Compare the colour of this wine with both the previous whites. Vouvray is often richer, more yellow. An off-dry, ripe example may well be slightly thicker, more weighty in texture.

AROMA Chenin Blanc grapes are often described as having an appley character – can you spot that in your wine? Try to pin down what sort of apples you find (green, yellow, ripe, baked, etc.). A nuttiness, especially walnut, may also be there, and what about honey? Does it smell sweet? If so, it may be an off-dry style.

FLAVOUR Look out for the same descriptors in the flavour. Do you like this wine? Not everyone enjoys Chenin Blanc – perhaps you agree with the famous 'wet wool' description – and both Chardonnay and Sauvignon tend to be more popular, but you might be seduced by a fine, fruity example. How are the acidity levels, and does this wine taste sweet or dry?

FINISH Compare the acidity and sense of youth on the finish of the wine. Does it seem to come from a cool or hot climate, and why? Assess its sweetness levels carefully. Vouvray is widely considered to be very food friendly, so what would you pair this wine with? Do you like it? Vouvray, especially off-dry styles, tends to divide opinion, so work out if this style of wine is for you.

4 Gewurztraminer from Alsace

APPEARANCE Your 'Gewurz' is likely to be the richest hued of this quartet – much more yellow and brightly coloured than the other wines. The grape has a rich yellowy pink colour when ripe – any pink hint here?

AROMA Take plenty of time over this one, as Gewurztraminer has a very distinctive bouquet, and once you've considered the aroma you should be able to spot it again easily in a blind tasting. It is usually described as 'spicy', but not chilli-spicy. It's more reminiscent of exotic eastern fragrances and cake spices, such as ginger, cardamon, rosewater and lychee. Some wines have peach, apricot and tangerine to the fore, others reek of Turkish Delight! Get going with some imaginative descriptions for this most heady and fragranced of grapes.

FLAVOUR It's important that Gewurztraminer has good, crisp acidity, or it might taste unsatisfying and unrefreshing. Look out for the exotic, unusual notes in the flavour. Think hard about texture (rich? Viscous?) and sweetness levels too, as it may be off-dry.

FINISH Is this wine balanced at the end? Do the fruitiness and acidity work together to create a harmonious, palatable wine, or is it out of kilter in one respect or another? This wine may impress you with its extrovert personality, but would you actually want to drink much of it?

What did you think?

As a group, did you enjoy the classic French whites?
Did they give you a glimpse of the wide variety of styles
made in that one country, or are you keen to get back to,
say, Chilean and Australian whites? Which grape variety
appealed the most and do you think these wines deserve
their classic status? Finally, an exercise in food and wine
matching. Here are four dishes – pair one of the wines to
each: Roast duck with apple sauce; mild goat's cheese
and tomato salad; fresh grilled salmon steaks; Thai
chicken and lemongrass stir-fry.

Sweet wines worlds apart

There are many weird and wonderful dessert wines made across the world, and choosing just four has been difficult. I hope a sampling of these delectable treats will banish any ideas of sickly, sugary gloop and make you want to go on to try plenty of other pudding wines!

You are tasting...

Sweet wine from the Bordeaux region of France
Preferably a Sauternes or Barsac, but Monbazillac or Saussignac would be cheaper, suitable substitutes. Sauternes and Barsac are pricey, but a half-bottle will probably do for your tasting.

Italian Vin Santo
Again, a half bottle should suffice. Pick a wine from the same year as the French sweet wine, if possible. The best Vin Santo comes from Tuscany.

New World sweet Semillon or Riesling
Choose a wine from Australia, New Zealand or Canada, as they make the best dessert wines of the newer wine-producing countries. Go for one from the same year (or close) and at a similar price.

Fortified French Muscat
Buy a Muscat de Rivesaltes, a Muscat de Beaumes-de-Venise or a Muscat de St-Jean de Minervois - fortified wines (with a little spirit added) from the south of the country. This wine may be cheaper, but go for a young, reasonably good-quality one.

Chill all these wines before tasting them. Taste from ordinary white wine glasses, with a small amount splashed into the bottom of each glass.

1 Sweet Bordeaux

APPEARANCE Think about comparing the sweet wine with dry whites when you examine it – does it seem any different in terms of colour, or, when you swirl the glass, texture? Does the liquid stick to the sides of the glass more when you swoosh it around?

AROMA Your first 'official' sniff of a pudding wine, so does the sweetness leap out of the glass? In what form – honey, marmalade, barleysugar etc? Does the wine smell fresh, crisp and inviting? What about the fruit aromas – do they appear to be similar to the fruit characters you have spotted in dry whites?

FLAVOUR A classic tasting note for Bordeaux sweet wine would probably include peach or apricot, honey or beeswax, some candied peel. Perhaps there is also something more obscure, that hints of noble rot (see page 102) – mushrooms, nuts or over-ripe, rotting fruit. Can you find any, or all, of these characteristics in this wine?

FINISH Think about the overall balance of the wine – the sweetness, the acidity (which should be fresh and tangy on the finish) and the fruit character. Does it work, or is it unbalanced? How long does the flavour linger on the tastebuds compared with the dry whites? Is it cloying or moreish?

2 Italian Vin Santo

APPEARANCE Compare with the French sweet wine. The Italian one may well be richer, more orange-amber in colour, but look and see for yourself. Contrast the texture too.

AROMA I gave you lots of pointers for the first wine, but think up the aroma descriptions for yourself here – this wine is made in a different place, from different grapes and in a slightly different way, so compare it with the French wine.

FLAVOUR Think about whether this wine is sweeter or drier, richer or lighter, fruitier or nuttier than the previous one. How is the acidity level here? Compare the wine not only with the other sweet wines that are in this tasting, but with dry whites. Is it just a matter of different levels of sweetness, or is there more going on here to define a sweet wine? For example, you may find in this tasting that the fruit flavours are less fresh, more like dried fruits.

FINISH Always assess the balance and consider concentration too – is this wine richer and more intense, long and lingering, or lighter? Would it go with the same desserts, chocolates and cheeses? How is the balance between sweetness and acidity on the finish?

3 New World sweet wine

APPEARANCE Some dessert wines made from Semillon are quite orange in colour, others are bright yellow. Look at yours and describe it, comparing it to the previous two. Rieslings should be lighter, more straw-coloured, but not nearly as pale as the dry versions.

AROMA There is a popularly held belief that all wines from new wine-producing regions are ultra-fruity, with ripe, rich fruit aromas and flavours to the fore. Is it true of this wine? If not, what can you sniff out instead? Nuts or cream? Toffee or toast? Mushrooms or honey? Let your descriptions run wild!

FLAVOUR Assess the flavours, thinking about the two wines you've already tried. Are they similar? Is the sugar/acid level the same? I don't know whether your wine is made from botrytised grapes or not, but do look for signs of it in the flavour.

FINISH Is there anything that gives away the provenance of this wine? Does it seems squeaky-clean, highly modern and fruity, the product of a new hi-tech winery? Or a hotter climate? Always think about the levels of sugar and acids on the finish of a sweet wine – is it elegantly balanced? How do you like this wine compared with the first two? Would you expect to pay more or less for it?

4 Fortified French Muscat

APPEARANCE Is there anything in the appearance of this wine that shows it is fortified? There may not be, but look at the colour and texture to answer the question – a richer colour or a thicker texture?

AROMA The aroma may be quite different here, for two reasons – firstly, the wine is fortified, and secondly, it is made from a grape with a very individual character. Try to pin down the differences between this wine and the trio that preceded it – is it really the 'odd one out', as you might expect? Muscat is often described as 'grapey' – can you see why?

FLAVOUR Does this wine seem stronger in alcohol, more intense and richer than the others? The grapes used to make it are not botrytised – can you tell? Which fruit flavours shine through? Perhaps there's a fresher, primary fruit flavour here (lemons and oranges). If so, do you like this bright style of pudding wine or do you prefer the more mushroomy, nutty, botrytis style of the previous samples?

FINISH Again, assess the strength and concentration of the wine. Also think about whether the Muscat grapes and the fortification have made a tarter or sweeter, more luscious or more lean wine than the others. Does this wine suit different dishes to the other three?

What did you think?

There's a small chance that sweet wines are still not for you, but I'd like to think this tasting has opened your mind to the sheer variety of flavours out there – not just when you compare these four wines, but also when you think about the different flavours, aromas and textures they conjure up compared with dry whites. When would you like to drink these wines – with rich hot puddings, fruit desserts, chocolate, cheeses (which ones?), or simply on their own?

Riesling a sense of place

Four wines all made from the Riesling grape, first encountered in Stage One. Back then, it was a case of tasting Riesling simply to spot the major characteristics of the grape. Now for a more sophisticated tasting of Riesling, in different styles and from various parts of Europe, examining this great variety in detail.

You are tasting...

Inexpensive Riesling from Germany or Eastern Europe

For once, I suggest you buy a very cheap bottle! Pick any young, dry Riesling from Europe. It will be a good comparison for the pricey wines that follow.

Young German Riesling from the Mosel region

Make sure your wine is young (from a very recent vintage) and is dry, or dry-ish – it should say the words *Trocken* and/or *Kabinett* on the label to indicate this. It will cost more.

Alsace Riesling from a grand cru site

French Riesling from the Alsace area – pick an equally young vintage and try to find a grand cru wine (one from a top vineyard site) so that you are trying one of the best, supposedly.

Sweet German or Austrian Riesling

Pick a wine (a half bottle will do just fine) that says Beerenauslese or Trockenbeerenauslese on the label, which indicates sweetness. Or you could splash out and buy an Eiswein. Make sure the label says Riesling.

Taste all these wines lightly chilled.

1 German or East European Riesling

APPEARANCE This will almost certainly appear very light, thin and colourless. Be suspicious if it is darker – it may be oxidised, or just plain nasty!

AROMA You should know by now what to expect from our previous tastings of Riesling – so be on the look-out for fresh, pure fruit aromas, probably citrus and apple, and perhaps something of the petrol and honey that can occur. How complex or simple is this wine?

FLAVOUR Quite probably this wine is no great shakes (although you never know...) but look out for crisp, refreshing flavours of fresh fruit, firm acidity, a mouth-cleansing finish. Oh, and note the lack of oakiness. Is this a wine of simple but delightful charms, one with which you would be happy to quench your thirst, or is it too bland for that? And think about how it compares with the Sauvignon Blanc and Pinot Grigio you have encountered. Would this score higher or lower with you on flavour?

FINISH Does this wine finish on a short, dull and disappointing note, or is it long and flavoursome? How are the acidity levels on the finish? And does it give a final impression of being sweet, medium or dry – always worth considering carefully with Riesling, which runs the gamut from luscious to bone-dry.

2 Young Mosel Riesling

APPEARANCE Compare with the previous wine, although there may not be much difference. Are there glints of straw, yellow or green in the pale colour?

AROMA Try to decide if this wine is more or less attractive than the previous one. Is there more to say about the aroma here? Mosel Rieslings have a delicate scent, but that's not the same as neutral or dull. The perfume should be noticeably appealing and fresh, and perhaps it will have a floral note (which flower?) along with the fruit.

FLAVOUR Bear in mind this is a subtle wine, but one that may have much more complexity or detail. Think about the floral/fruit character, a possible hint of honey and perhaps some mineral notes. Is it nicely balanced? Does it conjure up spring/summer days, as it should? Is this a more complex and sophisticated wine than the previous one?

FINISH I always think a good Mosel Riesling should have a succulent finish and be extremely moreish, so that you want another glass very much! Is this the case here? Can you tell that this wine has relatively low alcohol levels? If so, how? Is it light, fresh and clean on the finish?

3 Alsace Riesling from a grand cru site

APPEARANCE Alsace Riesling is generally richer and a little deeper in colour than German Riesling – but check this out for yourself and don't forget to swirl the liquid too, looking at its texture. Think hard about the clues that the wine's appearance lets slip.

AROMA Make a serious comparison here – you can expect a fuller scent, with somewhat different characteristics, despite the fact that the wine is made close to the German border. Are the fruit aromas the same?

FLAVOUR Again, this wine should form an interesting contrast with the previous duo. Think about how rich, full and concentrated it does or doesn't seem. Examine the fruit flavours, the level of honey/petrol, the mineral element, or lack of it. Go back and revisit the first two wines. There should be striking difference between those two and this one, so try to describe the contrast.

FINISH Note the acidity, sweetness and length of flavour. This wine comes from one of the top rated vineyards in Germany – does it seem like good quality to you? Would you seek it out and pay more money for it, compared with cheaper Alsace wines or the first inexpensive Riesling of this tasting?

4 Sweet German or Austrian Riesling

APPEARANCE Sweet wines are usually richer in colour than dry ones, so look out for that. However, this is Riesling and so it should not appear very rich. How yellow and bright is this wine, and does it seem more viscous?

AROMA It's fascinating to spot the changes in a wine when it is made from sweet, concentrated, botrytised grapes, as this has been. Compare the aroma with those of the three dry Rieslings. Can you spot different nuances, and what are they – candied peel, honey, marmalade, beeswax?

FLAVOUR Ditto for the flavour – try to pin down what, apart from the obvious sweetness, is different here. Think about the exact types of fruit, whether they seem like dried or candied fruits or fresh ones. Have any other complex nuances have crept into this one, and what is missing now?

FINISH Assess sweetness, length and that crucial acidity, as it is important the wine tastes fresh and crisp as well as honeyed. You have now encountered several dessert wines (see previous tasting), so do you think Riesling works well in a sweet style? Would you look forward to drinking sweet Riesling again, and would you be prepared to pay quite a steep price for it?

What did you think?

Do you now think that Riesling often gets an unjustly
bad press? It is a remarkable grape variety, offering a
wide range of delicious white wines, both sweet, medium
and dry (don't forget the New World Riesling we tried
earlier in the book, too). But you may not like it - it's up
to you. Try to decide, though, what it is that appeals or
not about Riesling - is it the high acidity, the delicate
fruit flavours, the lack of oak that makes it a winner, or
are you about to run screaming back to Chardonnay?
As usual, think about food matching - dream up some
delicate recipes to match these subtle wines.

Red classics

There are two wine-making regions of France which remain celebrated above all others. Is this adulation justified? Judge the styles and the standards for yourself, kicking off with these four reds from the most famous wine regions of all, Bordeaux and Burgundy.

You are tasting...

Beaujolais from southern Burgundy
Avoid the very cheapest, especially Beaujolais Nouveau. Find a young Beaujolais-Villages, or a wine from a named village in the area – Morgon, Fleurie or Moulin-à-Vent – made from the Gamay grape.

Classic red burgundy
A wine made from Pinot Noir, although the label will indicate the location of the vineyards, not the variety. Go for a medium-priced red burgundy that is reasonably young, and pick a classic site such as Gevrey-Chambertin or Nuits-St-Georges.

Red Bordeaux from the Médoc
Choose a Cabernet-rich blend, avoiding the cheap and expensive. Aim for a mid-priced, young Médoc red, preferably from the same year as the burgundy.

Merlot-based Bordeaux from St-Emilion
Over to the other side of the river – the 'Left Bank' – for a modern, fruity red Bordeaux. Pick a St-Emilion as the wine made here is mainly Merlot, or a Pomerol. Again, pick something that compares well in price and age with the wines above.

Taste all these wines at room temperature. You may want to decant the last three before tasting.

1 Beaujolais from southern Burgundy

APPEARANCE A good Beaujolais is a bright garnet, vivid and colourful. There shouldn't be any trace of brick-brown. Check out the texture too – probably quite light/thin compared with the others here.

AROMA The classic tasting note for Beaujolais, or indeed any wine made from the Gamay grape, is 'strawberry'. You might notice some other red fruits – cherries, plums – in there too, perhaps with a hint of marzipan and cream. Does the wine smell fresh, juicy and inviting, as it should? With luck it will conjure up high summer fruit-picking, but judge for yourself.

FLAVOUR Those fruity flavours should be fresh, tangy and clean-tasting. Notice how Beaujolais is an 'uncluttered' sort of wine – there is no subtle depth of spice, pepper or nuts, no oakiness and no heavy tannins.

FINISH Again, this should be a simple but pleasant experience – the Beaujolais must be refreshing and fruity, leaving a slight tang of succulent acidity in the mouth. It should be moreish and relatively light. Does yours measure up, or have you got a dud? Is this your style of wine or do you find it lacking some guts? Can you imagine drinking it lightly chilled, as I would? Decide if it would need food or if you could enjoy it on its own.

2 Classic red burgundy

APPEARANCE Burgundy changes its hue considerably with age, but a young wine should have plenty of bright ruby red colour. Check it against the previous wine for comparison.

AROMA Pinot Noir also has a red-berry aroma, but how does it differ from the scent of the Gamay? Look out for any other complexities and subtleties – nuts, cream, toffee – and any signs of oak ageing, such as spice or vanilla. Does it seem to be a more interesting wine than the Beaujolais at this stage?

FLAVOUR Carefully note the texture of this wine – it is an important quality of fine Pinot Noir that it is silky smooth, very rounded and moreish. Do the flavours major on fresh fruit, or is there much more going on here, perhaps some spice or nuttiness?

FINISH Think about acidity levels, that desirable roundness, softness of touch and whether the flavours linger. Has the oak been judged correctly, or is it too obvious or, indeed, too light? Is this wine as harmonious and seductive as burgundy is reputed to be? Is it that much better than the supposedly more humble Beaujolais? Red burgundy can be quite expensive, so on this early assessment, do you think you'd be prepared to explore some more pricey bottles or rather save your money for different styles of red wine?

3 Red Bordeaux from the Médoc

APPEARANCE Cabernet tends to yield up a deeper colour than many reds, so how does the shade of this wine measure up against the previous two? Does it look richer, more full-bodied, and if so, in what way?

AROMA Is the tell-tale aroma of blackcurrant (cassis) there in your wine? What about some of the more eclectic tasting notes often applied to claret - lead pencil, mint, cedar? Does the wine seem oaky?

FLAVOUR Would you describe this wine as rich, fruity and generous, or more austere and restrained than the burgundy? Think about texture again - how does it compare in terms of softness/richness and tannin levels? Are those flavours typical of Cabernet, with cassis at the very core?

FINISH You may find it easier to assess tannin and richness on the finish than on the immediate flavour. Does this wine leave you with a 'furry', or 'chewy' tannic sensation in the mouth? Is that OK, or would you prefer to see it soften with age? Would you match it with light or rich food? How would you compare the overall character of the wine with first the Beaujolais, then the red burgundy? Try to imagine perfect moments to open each of these three wines - summer parties, winter Sunday roasts or Christmas turkey?

4 Merlot-based St-Emilion Bordeaux

APPEARANCE Which of the three previous wines does this one most look like? How would you describe the exact shade of red - does it seem to be a youthful colour? How rich and dense is the texture?

AROMA Merlot has a reputation for being more generously fruity than Cabernet, but is this borne out by the scent of this wine? Does it display lots of ripe red berry fruit? How do the aromas differ from the red berries you encountered in the Beaujolais and burgundy?

FLAVOUR Does this wine seem more 'approachable' than the previous one - is it less tannic and more softly fruity and round? Does it seem more modern, like a wine from a New World country, such as Australia or Chile? Think about the contrast between this claret and the previous one - decide whether it is more or less tannic, more or less complex.

FINISH Assess the tannin levels here, and how long the flavour lingers. Think particularly about the oak element, compared with the third wine. Which of the two Bordeaux reds do you think would keep the longest, unopened and stored in a cellar? Are the differences between this wine and the previous one subtle, or quite marked? Would you imagine (if you didn't know) that they came from the same region of France? And if so, why?

What did you think?

Rather than ranking these wines, it's perhaps more useful to decide which one suits which occasion: very lightly chilled on a hot summer's day; paired with soft cheeses; to go with Christmas roast etc. Do work out if you think the wines are good value for money. Which ones would keep well, and for how long? One of these reds needs drinking up earlier than the rest – which one? Finally, try to compare them with the other reds you have sampled in earlier tastings, especially the Australian Shiraz, the Rhône red, the Italian and Spanish wines. You might find you need your tasting notes to help you, but try to remember the flavours and aromas without prompting...

New wave reds a bright future

Here are four red wines that can be classified as 'new wave'. They are not necessarily new on the scene – the southern Italian red has been made in a similar style for centuries – but they have only recently become popular on the international stage. All four are proving successful with a new generation of wine drinkers. Let's call them 'modern classic reds', shall we?

You are tasting...

Argentinian Malbec
It may have been a French grape originally, but it took the Argentinians to put Malbec on the map. In South America, and particularly around the Mendoza area of Argentina, Malbec is making a splash. Pick a medium-priced, fairly young wine.

Southern Italian Red
Southern Italy is less well known for its wine. Now Sicily and the regions of Puglia, Calabria and Campania have given us riper, softer reds made from indigenous grapes like Primitivo, Negroamaro and Nero d'Avola. Pick a low-priced red from here.

Californian Zinfandel
Widely believed to be the same grape as Primitivo, Zinfandel is grown almost exclusively in California, making weak blush rosé, as well as rich reds. Go for a true red, medium priced.

South African Pinotage
The Western Cape's very own grape variety, created from a Cinsaut and Pinot Noir cross in the 1920s. Trade up from the rougher, thinner cheapies and aim for a medium-priced gem. One from the Stellenbosch region would be a good bet.

Serve all wines at room temperature.

1 Argentinian Malbec

APPEARANCE Work out how deep or light in colour this wine is, compared with other reds you have tried along the way. Try to describe the colour accurately – brick red, deep purple, mahogany, etc.

AROMA Many liken the scent of Malbec to black cherry, and I have found a host of other black and red fruits there too. Try to identify more than one fruit in this cocktail of aromas, and do look out for signs of oakiness – spice, coconut, vanilla – and other nuances such as toasted nuts or chocolate. Is this wine inviting? Does it seem rich?

FLAVOUR Those black cherries should shine through! Argentina, like Chile, is capable of very fruity reds with a pure, fresh summer pudding taste, but does this wine fit that description? Is it rich and ripe, or lean and light? And can you taste any oak? Think about this wine in contrast with reds that have gone before – the Spanish and Italian wines of Stage Two, for example. Does it taste significantly new and exciting?

FINISH How long and concentrated are the flavours? Did you notice much tannin? What about acidity levels and sweetness? Consider the length of time the flavours linger, and whether the finish is well-balanced overall. Are you left with a very strong impression of fresh fruitiness?

2 Southern Italian red

APPEARANCE Compare this wine with the previous one and note its age while doing so – an older Italian red will be brick-brown-red, while a young one should look more bluey-purple. How dense is the colour and texture?

AROMA It certainly should be aromatic, with plenty to draw you in and make you want to taste the wine later. Try to pin down what can be quite unusual aromas – Italian reds always seem to have interesting, different smells. What about chocolate or herbs, tealeaves or pepper?

FLAVOUR How rounded, mouthfilling and/or tannic is this wine? Is it as overtly fruity (primary fruits) as the previous one? Describe the fruits you find and note whether there are dried fruits here too – prunes, figs, raisins – as this can be typical of wines from an area as hot as southern Italy.

FINISH Assess the overall quality – southern Italian reds have improved but there are still plenty of disappointing examples. Compare the acidity, oakiness (or otherwise) and concentration with that of the previous wine. Do you like the rather unusual character of this red? The Italians pride themselves on making good 'food' wines, so think of one or two dishes that this would complement.

3 Californian Zinfandel

APPEARANCE This grape is known to produce reds with plenty of bright ruby colour – check this out in your glass. How does it look compared with the previous two wines? Is it richer or lighter?

AROMA I often find raspberries in Zinfandel, but it depends somewhat on the producer – and the taster! Some examples are much richer and have 'blacker' fruit – blackberries, cassis and so on – and look out for overtly spicy oak and a twist of pepper in some examples.

FLAVOUR How rich is your 'Zin'? Does it major on fresh fruit flavours or is it darker, wilder, somehow more exotic? Check the acidity levels, which can be rasping sometimes, and that the oak and tannins seem to be in balance. Would you classify this as a light, medium or full-bodied red?

FINISH Can you spot the oak here? How fruitily ripe and fulsome is it? Compare the finish to the other wines, thinking especially about specific fruit flavours, sweetness and acidity. Would you have guessed this came from a hot or cool climate wine region? Give reasons for your answer. Try to decide how much you like this wine – would you want to drink more than one glass of it?

4 South African Pinotage

APPEARANCE By now you should be an expert in describing the various shades of red wine! Put this wine into the colour spectrum – purple, bluey, brick, mahogany, garnet?

AROMA The style of Pinotage varies considerably – it may be light, fruity and plummy, or big, chunky and oaked. Poorer examples are described as rough and 'tomatoey'; great ones have layers of fresh purple berries, chocolate, cream and spicy oak. Try to assess your wine from its aroma alone before tasting it.

FLAVOUR Acidity can be a problem here – does your wine have too little, too much, or is it just right? How appealing are the fruit flavours? Assess the level of oakiness compared to the previous three wines. Look in particular at the balance of flavours – Pinotage can sometimes be a little rough and acidic, so make sure yours works as a complete and satisfying mouthful!

FINISH Time to decide whether you like Pinotage more or less than the other wines you've tasted here. This will depend partly on the quality of the wine you bought. Have you got a delicious, true, modern, new wave classic, or does this wine simply taste like Cape reds of the past – rough and sour?

What did you think?

We've already come across plenty of classic European reds (claret, red burgundy, Chianti, Rioja), so how does this quartet fit in with them? Better, or worse? Have exciting new flavours and aromas been revealed or would you give these styles of red a wide berth in the future? Work out what was most interesting about each one - perhaps an unusual aroma or a particularly rounded texture. Are these serious dinner party wines or merely party plonk?

Port, sherry and Madeira

Make sure you have read the section on fortified wines (page 107) before starting this tasting. Be prepared for some very different scents and flavours, not to mention textures, from these wines. Don't expect an onslaught of primary fruits. Instead, be open to the unusual, the exotic – dried fruits, nuts, spices, toffee, even a salty tang... In the heady world of fortified wines, anything can happen!

You are tasting...

Dry, pale sherry
Today, sherry can only say 'sherry' on the label if it comes from the Andalucia region of Spain, so don't worry about getting the Real Thing – it will be if it says the 'Sh...' word! Choose a fino or manzanilla style, and buy a new bottle.

Tawny port
From the Douro Valley in Portugal, tawny port should be poured from a new bottle. Pick a ten-year-old tawny to get quality without breaking the bank. A half-bottle will be enough for four tasters.

Red port
Avoid bog-standard 'ruby' or the only-slightly-better 'vintage character' red, and buy an LBV (Late-Bottled-Vintage) port. Buy new – don't raid an old bottle. Again, consider buying a half bottle.

Malmsey Madeira
There are several styles of Madeira – malmsey is the sweetest. Don't accept a substitute that says 'rich, sweet' Madeira – the word 'Malmsey' should be on the label. A half bottle should suffice.

Serve the dry sherry chilled, the tawny very lightly chilled, the red port and Madeira at room temperature. No need to decant before tasting.

1 Dry, pale sherry

APPEARANCE Think of sherry, and many imagine a deep amber, sticky appearance. Sweeter, richer styles have this, but note how pale and thin this dry style is. How does it compare in looks with ordinary dry white table wine?

AROMA Dry, pale sherry should smell fresh, fresh, fresh. The perfume should give the impression of being young, vibrant and mouthwatering. Look out for a lemon zest aroma, and perhaps green olives in brine. There may be some breadiness/doughiness too, from the yeast blanket which has formed on it. Notice how strong the aroma is.

FLAVOUR The same characteristics should be on the flavour – a refreshing crispness, a lemon fruitiness and a salty tang. Assess the effects of the *flor* yeast again – is there a rich, bready note? How acidic is this wine?

FINISH If dry sherry doesn't make your mouth water, there's something wrong with it. Notice the very fresh finish, the acidity levels and the dryness. Decided how long the flavour lingers, compared with ordinary white table wines. Indeed, if you usually like dry whites, do you like this too? And for the same reasons? Try to work out exactly what it is you like or dislike here, compared with dry white wines.

2 Tawny port

APPEARANCE Another surprising hue, if you had thought all ports were deep red. Tawny is aged in oak barrels for years before release, and has a brownish, amber colour – tawny, in fact! Check out the viscosity of the liquid.

AROMA You might find some fresh fruit here (I often find oranges on the aroma) but there's so much more going on. Toffee, nuts (which ones?), dried peel, chocolate and cream should start you off, but see what else is in this mature, intricate aroma. Can you sniff out the fact that it is a richly fortified wine? Does it smell sweet?

FLAVOUR And does it taste sweet? What about a tang of acidity – is it there, and does it make the wine seem well-balanced? Try to describe the rich, weighty texture of the wine, as well as its fruit flavours and other attributes, such as a toasty nuttiness.

FINISH The flavour of all port should linger on the tongue for ages, and give you a complex finish of many layers. Chocolate? Caramel? Nuts? How is the sweetness, and is there also a fresh acidity, or is the end result just too sickly? Can you imagine enjoying this port served very chilled? Think about the time you would want to drink this – with pudding, or cheese, or on its own?

3 Red port

APPEARANCE Compare this closely with the tawny port. It will certainly be redder, but you should also look at the density of colour and the thickness of the wine when you swirl it around the glass.

AROMA This wine should have plenty of rich aroma. As well as red berry fruit, there should be cherries, fruitcake, spices such as cloves and cinnamon, and perhaps a hint of plain chocolate too. See if your wine measures up, or if it just smells disappointingly simple and fruity.

FLAVOUR LBV should show a fine red style without the need to age and without the heavy tannin of a true vintage port. Again, a simple blast of red fruit is not enough. Port should taste sweet, with red cherries and fruitcake, and lots of more subtle nuances, from spice to chocolate. Think about the richness and the concentration of flavour, and whether it is more or less tannic than the tawny.

FINISH Think again about tannin levels, acidity and sweetness, particularly in comparison with the tawny port. Is this a richly concentrated wine? Would you drink this on the same occasions as a tawny? And would this suit being served cold, or at room temperature? Which food would you match with it – red meats, hard cheeses, puddings or nuts?

4 Malmsey Madeira

APPEARANCE Compare the colour with wines two and three. Is it as brown as the tawny port, or as red as the LBV? What about the texture – when you swirl it around the glass, do long trails of it dribble slowly down the sides? What might this tell you?

AROMA Madeira is made in a special way which involves heating the wine – does this show at all in the aroma? It might smell a little burnt or caramelised. What else is in the fragrance? Is it more like the oak-aged tawny port, or the fruitier red port?

FLAVOUR Assess the sweetness, the fruit character, and the roundness and richness of the wine. Does that 'cooked' character come across on the flavour? Are there any more unusual nuances here? How much do you like this wine, compared to the other fortified ones?

FINISH Do you think this wine is well-balanced – does it have enough acidity or 'tang' to match the sweetness? How sweet is the finish relative to the other wines? Does a different flavour come through on the end of the mouthful – say, a nuttiness, a creaminess or a spiciness? How intense and lingering are the flavours? Madeira is often used for cooking – can you think of any sauces or gravies or soups that could be enhanced by a splash of this wine? Or is it perhaps too delicious to waste in the kitchen?

What did you think?

The pale, dry sherry is clearly quite a different creature to the other three fortified wines, so start by deciding if you liked that and when you might want to drink it. Did it make sense to chill it before serving? As for the other wines, they are more similar in character, but examine the subtle shifts in flavour, texture and finish between them. Think about the characteristics that have shone through in this tasting, compared to a tasting of dry red wines. Do you enjoy this style of wine, overall, or does fortified wine deserve its 'fuddy-duddy' reputation? When would you want to drink a tawny, an LBV and a sweet Madeira?

Buyer's guide

More here on how to get the most out of shopping for wine. At this advanced stage, we move on to consider whether you need to read endless columns and books about wine; whether fashionable labels are worth all the fuss (and money) and how to buy wine at auction...

Good advice: At home

No one individual wine writer should dictate your taste in wine – it's better to discover that for yourself. So this book focuses on tasting exercises and making your own way, rather than telling you what to think. If a critic regularly steers you towards the sort of bottles that suit you, fine. Read his or her column, buy his or her books and take on board the recommendations. Just don't think of any wine critic as a 'guru' – we all have different tastes in wine.

You don't need a huge library of books, but it helps to keep up with the latest news from wine regions. Reading a regular wine column in a good paper and/or purchasing an annual wine guide with vintage reports are sensible ways to do this. Remember that wine books focusing on the latest 'best buys' or the latest vintage news go out of date as quickly as a bottle of fragile rosé! You may find an annual guide to buying wine, such as the UK's *Which? Wine Guide*, helpful in deciding which wine merchants to use. Note when they have special offers, or if there are opportunities to taste instore or attend wine events – anything to help you get to know fine wine well.

Labels: Classic styles

Generally, you pay pretty hefty prices for these types of wine, but they come into their own as great buys once you avoid so-called bargains in the same categories. Put simply, cheap red Bordeaux, knock-down Piedmont reds and so on tend to be awful, so be prepared to shell out! I'm reluctant to list the cult labels from Australia, California and New Zealand, as it's a shame to pander to fashionable wineries, but such labels do exist, and you might lust after them. Do taste them before parting with your money.

Use a vintage chart to be sure you get wine from the best years – although with experience you may spot an under-rated year in a particular region and find you enjoy the wines very much. The same goes for producers – pick a reputable name (a high street guide will help, as will a good merchant) but if you find an obscure label you like, go for it. Make sure you taste before buying in quantity.

Shop alternatives: Wine auctions

There is an old adage in the trade that says in order to make a small fortune out of wine, you need to start with a large one. That holds true whether you are starting a vineyard, a wine shop or a collection for investment. Well, it's nearly always true. You may be lucky enough to buy a case of decent claret from a recent vintage and find its price soars over time. However, to make a profit you will need to keep it in exactly the right conditions, sell it at the right time (before its quality or reputation drops, or more of it floods the market), and, if it's in your own home, you must be seriously disciplined not to drink it yourself! And as a fine wine lover, how can you resist the latter? Ironically, investing in wine is harder for wine connoisseurs than for anyone else, as we are so easily tempted to pull the cork and sample our precious stock. If you must try investing in wine instead of drinking it, first consult a specialist merchant, like Farr Vintners, Berry Brothers, Justerini and Brooks in London.

Buying wine at auction is not a bad idea, if you have the time and inclination to travel to major auction houses, or trade on-line or by phone. It can be an exciting way to get hold of fine, rare wine, and very mature wine in particular, which seldom appears in shops. Do careful research, to get an idea of the condition of very old bottles. Some outlets deal in mature bottles which might repay further cellaring, while venerable wine sold at auction may need drinking up soon, or might simply be trading on a glamorous past.

Serious drinkers may buy wine at auction to keep in their cellar, collecting fine and rare wines.

RUSTENBERG
RUSTENBERG
WINE OF ORIGIN STELLE
KEN FORRESTER SCHOLTZENHOF
RUSTENBERG
SPRINGFIELD ESTATE
PINOTAGE
SHIRAZ

Drinker's guide

In an ideal world, all wine lovers would build up a collection of wonderful wines. The styles would be so varied that there would be something special to suit every occasion. If that's your aim (and why not?), then here's how to find brilliant, one-off food matches, equip the perfect cellar and, finally, spot the odd fault like a pro!

Food matching: 'Different' mixes

You know quite a lot about food and wine matching now – the sensible partners, at any rate – so what about some really exciting, eclectic, off-beat marriages? Try dry sherry with sushi; Malbec with chocolate; tawny port and chocolate mousse; off-dry Gewurztraminer and sweet and sour Chinese chicken; unoaked Chardonnay with eggs (a tricky food to match with wine); and the classic but too-rarely attempted Sauternes (or other botrytis dessert wine) with smooth pâtés or Roquefort cheese.

Storage: Cellaring

How do you equip the perfect cellar for keeping fine wine? For many, it will be a case of finding a cellar at all. The basement is a good place to store wine as it is cool, dark and quiet, but make sure it has no really smelly products in there, such as paint or white spirit, as their pungent aromas can affect wine. Garages tend to be too cold and petrolly, so if you don't have a cellar/basement, try the cupboard under the stairs, a disused cupboard far away from radiators and ovens, or an old cloakroom. I know someone who uses a downstairs toilet for storing wine, another who has a temperature-controlled outbuilding, and yet another who stores wine under the big bed in his cool, airy spare room. In my book, the kitchen is the worst place for long-term storage of wine – the temperature fluctuates too much. If you can't find anywhere suitable, you could invest in a temperature-controlled storage unit (effective but expensive), or keep your wine with a firm of wine storage specialists, who will ensure it's kept correctly.

Wine racks won't fit under a bed, but for any other space, invest in a set of them. You can have them made bespoke to fit your cellar/downstairs cupboard space, or just buy and saw them to fit. Wooden racks are better than metal ones, as metal often snags the wine's label. You can leave your wine on its side in the cases in which it arrives – it will come to no harm like this, but you may find it hard to keep track of the amount you have and where it is.

Make sure your cellar/cupboard has a light that you can switch on when you need to, but otherwise keep your wine in the dark. Turn off any radiators in the storage space. If you think the air is particularly dry, place a big bowl of water there – the water will evaporate gradually, providing more humidity. You can invest in a fancy cellar design, designer racks, a small tasting table and chairs, but you don't have to – it won't affect the quality of the wine!

It is certainly frustrating to lose track of a fine wine you have collected, only to discover it is past it when you open it. If you have a large collection of fine wines, it pays to keep it in good order and have a record somewhere. This might mean keeping a cellar log, listing all your wines and stating when and where they were bought, the vintages and the date of optimum drinking. If you buy a case of one particular wine and start opening a bottle or two, note what it tastes like and whether it needs drinking up or cellaring for longer. Special tags that hang on the bottle necks, where you can write the name, the vintage and the date of purchase, are helpful. If in doubt about a wine's suitability for drinking, do open it, as it will be worse if it has 'gone over' than if it is a little too young.

Serving: Spotting faulty wine

By now, sadly, you may well have come across a corked wine (see page 23) – one infected by a mouldy bark cork, which leaves a distinctly musty aroma or flavour in the wine. Some wines are overtly, flagrantly corked and the 'cork taint' character is quite distinct. Others have a more subtle problem – the fruit flavour and freshness are muted, dampened down, and it may seem as though you simply have a boring, uninspiring wine in your glass. In this instance, if you leave your wine opened for long enough, its true mustiness will start to come out.

It's hard to know exactly how many bottles of wine are corked. Obviously, those with screw-caps or plastic stoppers shouldn't suffer from this problem, but for those with natural corks, I think about one in fifteen is tainted. Others estimate a higher incidence of around one in ten, while cork supporters boast of only one in two hundred being corked. Whatever the case, it is a shame the cork industry has not come up with a dead-cert way to ensure cork taint never happens. Until it does, consumers will look for alternative closures, and who can blame them?

Another fault to look out for is oxidation, where air has got into the bottle and spoilt the wine, as when an apple turns brown and mushy once exposed to air. A wine that has been over-sulphured has a smell like a struck match, and can cause wheezing and allergic reaction. If you have a faulty wine, don't pour it away; reseal it and take it back to the shop, or send it back in a restaurant, and ask for a replacement. Incidentally, small white crystals in a bottle are tartrate deposits and are harmless, not affecting the flavour of the wine. As for sediment, that is harmless too.

Moving on

Don't leave things here. To keep up with the fast pace of the wine world, that means continuing to taste wine on a regular basis. Stop now, and you'll miss out, as everyone's taste in wine should gradually evolve. Here's how to learn more...

Please don't finish this book with the sense that you have covered the entire subject of wine! It is intended as a practical introduction to an extremely complicated yet enjoyable topic, and anyway, all the information and tastings in the world wouldn't cover the variety of wine. That's because each new year brings a whole new crop of wines, quite unlike any others. It's one of the fascinating things about the liquid – each new release is a different creature waiting to be discovered. Then there are the newly planted vineyards, newly established regions, upcoming winemakers, developments in technology and evolutions in style which change the face of wine each decade. You have to run – or at the very least trot – to keep up with it all.

But if the information here, and your experiences of tasting wine, have inspired you to continue a vinous love affair (and I hope they have), here's where to go next:

Adopt a wine merchant...

I can't over-estimate the value of a friendly and knowledgeable wine merchant. Get to know a reputable one and he or she should introduce you to many wines that suit your style of drinking. Make the most of the tips you receive – not just how to part with your money, but how to deepen your wine wisdom.

How about getting the merchant to suggest a mixed case of wines that are new to you, but are selected with an eye on your preferred tastes? Make sure you know about any tasting events or wine dinners that are being planned by the shop. You could even try to persuade him or her to open a few bottles one evening for you and your bunch of wine-crazy friends. The best merchants for this are likely to be small, independent outlets that stock up with wines from interesting producers. The huge multiple retailers and supermarkets simply can't compete with this sort of personal attention.

Join a club...

By which I mean a local, amateur group of wine fanciers. You may have formed your own small network of wine buffs already, but there are usually larger associations that meet regularly to taste wine and have dinner. Bigger groups have more clout when it comes to inviting winemakers to speak, so try to get to some tutored tastings too. Write directly to winemakers, or email them, or approach them through their importers (details are on the back label of many bottles) and ask them to give talks for free. You may well strike lucky on their next trip to your area, especially if you offer to put them up and feed them! If not, try a wine merchant or even (dare I say it) a wine writer. But winemakers should be your priority, as they are naturally the most illuminating about their region, their fruit and their methods.

Read around the subject...

Consider subscribing to a wine magazine. These are usually monthly publications that carry the latest wine news, up-to-date vintage assessments, detailed features about wine regions and profiles of winemakers. Do bear in mind that sometimes the editorial content seems rather close to the advertising income! Just keep an independent mind when it comes to the most talked-up wines (you may not like it, even though 'World of Wine' says it's great) and you will certainly find something of interest in most issues. I'm talking about the well-established, major wine magazines here – every corner of the world will have some less well-known reads too.

Keep track of some newspaper wine columns too (again, stick to your own views and don't trust anyone else's tastebuds to reflect yours completely). And buy a few wine books (see pages 104 and 134). Go for books on vintages, and perhaps one or two on specific wine regions that appeal to you before anything else. Splash out on one big encyclopaedia of wine, if you can, as it should answer many one-off, niggly questions that crop up. I recommend *The Oxford Companion to Wine*.

Take a test...

This book has given you a course to complete in your own house (or your friends' houses). If you want to continue tasting wine on a 'course' basis, there are numerous wine classes that you can take outside the home. These will vary in quality, expense and convenience. Make sure you compare several on offer in your town before joining one. Some courses can be pricey, especially when you throw in the cost of travel to and from them, so make sure you do your research before committing. When you make enquiries about a course, ask about the wines you will be tasting. The fee should reflect the price of the wines that will be opened during the classes, so are they widely available, cheap and cheerful bottles, or will some serious bottles be sampled? If possible, get a feel for the tutor's style of teaching by chatting to him or her on the phone. The best wine courses are usually discovered by personal recommendation from a friend, and they tend to be the most fun and sociable, as well as the most instructive.

If you are really serious about wine, and perhaps even considering a job in wine retail, then take a set of exams. The Wine and Spirit Education Trust, based in London, is the major educator for the wine trade in the UK, but keen amateurs can also join its courses. In 2002, 11,000 people sat exams, from the basic foundation course up various steps to the fearsome diploma. These candidates came from 24 different countries, so don't worry if you don't live in London. Take a look at the WSET website (www.wset.co.uk) for further information. I recommend these courses, but be aware that they are serious, and even rather gruelling at the advanced end, so they are not for everyone.

Travel widely...

The tastings in this book have launched you into a lifetime of sampling new and exciting wines. Although these were set in the context of home tasting, I admit there is an even better way to get to know wine. Travelling to wine regions and tasting bottles in situ, at the cellar door, is a wonderful way to experience wine. There is nothing, absolutely nothing, like a wine tasting holiday to inspire and instruct. There can be moments of true revelation in such expeditions – imagine sitting in the Chilean sunshine, tasting wines from vines growing right by your feet. Suddenly everything about a wine can make perfect sense – after all, the way it tastes, as you have learned, comes directly from the climate, the *terroir*, the style of the winery. I hope you experience such moments. Happy tasting!

Index Figures in *italics* refer to illustration captions

Acknowledgements

Thanks to the team at Quadrille, especially to Jane O'Shea for her major input on the original concept for this book, to Lisa Pendreigh for the unenviable task of goading me on and to Jane Keskeys for editing my words. More thanks to Tim and Charmaine for lovely, original photography and to Jim Smith for his expert art direction and design. But, above all, I must raise my glass to Ian, Alex and William for putting up with me while I wrote another book!

All special photography by Tim Winter, except those on pages 16, 17, 18, 20, 23, 61, 63, 64, 67, 93, 102, 105, 106, 109, 135 by Charmaine Grieger.